Skills in Language 1

REVISED EDITION

PREPARED BY EDUCATIONAL SYSTEMS CORPORATION

CAMBRIDGE
THE ADULT EDUCATION COMPANY
New York • Toronto

CONTENTS

THE PURPOSE OF THIS BOOK

This book will help you understand how words are put together to make good sentences. It will give you practice working with nouns and verbs and many other kinds of words that you use every day. Some words fit in certain sentences better than others do. Some words change when they are moved from one part of a sentence to another. Others change when they describe a thing or person or when they show the time at which something happened. There are certain rules that words follow when they are put together into sentences, and you will learn about the rules in this book. There are also certain rules that will help you spell words correctly. You will learn them, too.

Each chapter helps you learn in three ways. First you will learn about a certain kind of word and how it is used. Examples are given to help you understand. Then you will work a practice exercise called "Try It." There you will work with sentences that deal with that particular kind of word. You will also work another kind of practice exercise called "Try It in a Paragraph."

After you have studied many kinds of sentences, you can practice all the things you have learned by working the review exercises in Chapter 26.

The test sentences in Chapter 1 will show you your strengths and your weaknesses. They include the different kinds of word or sentence problems that are explained in the chapters of this book. After you have done the test sentences, check your answers on page 12.

1. HOW MUCH DO YOU KNOW ALREADY?

Read each sentence below. Decide whether or not the underlined word or words are used correctly. If they are used incorrectly, choose the correct word or words from the choices lettered (a) to (d) on the right-hand side of the page. Blacken the space next to the letter choice you make. Choice (a) is always the same as the underlined word or words in the sentence. When the word is used correctly in the sentence, blacken the space next to choice (a).

When you finish all the sentences, check your answers on pages 11–12. Next to each correct answer on page 12 is the chapter number in the book where you will find that answer explained.

Take as much time as you need to finish. Skip those sentences you aren't sure of, but mark them wrong when you check your answers.

LEARNING GOALS:
- To find out which language skills you need to practice

1. Sara went into the store, and <u>it</u> bought a pair of shoes.

   1. (a)|| it
     (b)|| she
     (c)|| they
     (d)|| he

2. She <u>pick</u> cherries in Wisconsin.

   2. (a)|| pick
     (b)|| picks
     (c)|| picking
     (d)|| pick's

3. Right now, I <u>wash</u> the dog.

   3. (a)|| wash
     (b)|| washed
     (c)|| am washing
     (d)|| was washing

4. <u>They</u> buys bananas.

   4. (a)|| They
     (b)|| We
     (c)|| He
     (d)|| I

5. She <u>will goes</u> tomorrow.

5. (a) | | will goes

   (b) | | is go

   (c) | | will go

   (d) | | wills go

6. Hector <u>went</u> tomorrow.

6. (a) | | went

   (b) | | will goes

   (c) | | will go

   (d) | | wents

7. I <u>will sneeze.</u>

7. (a) | | will sneeze.

   (b) | | am sneeze.

   (c) | | is sneeze.

   (d) | | will sneezed.

8. He <u>blowed</u> his horn.

8. (a) | | blowed

   (b) | | blew

   (c) | | blews

   (d) | | will blew

9. Maria answered <u>soft</u>.

9. (a) | | soft

   (b) | | softed

   (c) | | softing

   (d) | | softly

10. They <u>done</u> it a few minutes ago.

10. (a) | | done

    (b) | | do

    (c) | | does

    (d) | | did

11. I <u>is</u> happy.

11. (a) | | is

(b) | | am

(c) | | are

(d) | | were

12. <u>She</u> was happy last week.

12. (a) | | She

(b) | | You

(c) | | They

(d) | | We

13. The men <u>will been</u> happy.

13. (a) | | will been

(b) | | will being

(c) | | will be

(d) | | be

14. The bill came. <u>He</u> had "For sale of food" written on it.

14. (a) | | He

(b) | | It

(c) | | They

(d) | | Its

15. Neither Jesse nor his brother <u>are</u> sure.

15. (a) | | are

(b) | | is

(c) | | were

(d) | | be

16. He <u>has worked</u> there until last year.

16. (a) | | has worked

(b) | | have worked

(c) | | worked

(d) | | is working

17. <u>Its</u> raining.

17. (a)| | Its

    (b)| | It

    (c)| | Its'

    (d)| | It's

18. Elmer <u>don't</u> want it.

18. (a)| | don't

    (b)| | doesn't

    (c)| | do not

    (d)| | isn't

19. What <u>kind of a</u> place is this?

19. (a)| | kind of a

    (b)| | kind a

    (c)| | kind of

    (d)| | kind a of

20. Go and <u>lay down</u> for a while.

20. (a)| | lay down

    (b)| | lie down

    (c)| | laid down

    (d)| | lain down

21. Are you <u>sure</u>.

21. (a)| | sure.

    (b)| | sure!

    (c)| | sure?

    (d)| | sure,

22. There <u>is</u> your tools.

22. (a)| | is

    (b)| | be

    (c)| | was

    (d)| | are

23. Anybody who <u>wants</u> my car can have it.

23. (a) | | wants

    (b) | | will wants

    (c) | | want

    (d) | | has want

24. One of the detectives <u>look</u> for fingerprints.

24. (a) | | look

    (b) | | will looked

    (c) | | looks

    (d) | | has look

25. Malcolm X was born on <u>May, 19, 1925.</u>

25. (a) | | May, 19, 1925.

    (b) | | May, 19 1925.

    (c) | | May 19 1925.

    (d) | | May 19, 1925.

26. Just <u>between</u> the three of us, he's wrong.

26. (a) | | between

    (b) | | with

    (c) | | among

    (d) | | for

27. Andrea and Pete <u>likes</u> folk rock music.

27. (a) | | likes

    (b) | | like

    (c) | | had like

    (d) | | has liked

28. I had a sandwich, a glass of <u>milk, and</u> a piece of cake for lunch.

28. (a) | | milk, and

    (b) | | milk and

    (c) | | , milk and

    (d) | | milk, and,

29. He fooled <u>hisself</u>.

29. (a)| | hisself.

    (b)| | himself.

    (c)| | theirself.

    (d)| | myself.

30. It's <u>me</u>.

30. (a)| | me.

    (b)| | her.

    (c)| | I.

    (d)| | him.

31. I don't think it was <u>him</u> who did it.

31. (a)| | him

    (b)| | it

    (c)| | his

    (d)| | he

32. Listen, between <u>you and me</u>, she's lying.

32. (a)| | you and me,

    (b)| | she and I,

    (c)| | you and I,

    (d)| | them and I,

33. Don't give it to <u>her or I</u>.

33. (a)| | her or I.

    (b)| | she or I.

    (c)| | she or me.

    (d)| | her or me.

34. I <u>can't hardly</u> believe her.

34. (a)| | can't hardly

    (b)| | can hardly

    (c)| | can't not

    (d)| | can't do nothing but

35. <u>They</u> doesn't drink.

35. (a)| | They

    (b)| | He

    (c)| | We

    (d)| | I

36. <u>They're</u> ours.

36. (a)| | They're

    (b)| | There

    (c)| | Their

    (d)| | Here

37. <u>Who's</u> coat is this?

37. (a)| | Who's

    (b)| | Whose

    (c)| | Who'se

    (d)| | Whos

38. Before he went, he <u>had had</u> a cup of coffee.

38. (a)| | had had

    (b)| | has had

    (c)| | have

    (d)| | have had

39. <u>I don't know nothing.</u>

39. (a)| | I don't know nothing.

    (b)| | I don't know anything.

    (c)| | I don't hardly know.

    (d)| | I don't scarcely know nothing.

40. I dieted all <u>Spring</u> and <u>Winter</u> so I could wear a bikini in the <u>Summer</u>.

40. (a)| | Spring . . . Winter . . . Summer.

    (b)| | spring . . . Winter . . . Summer.

    (c)| | spring . . . winter . . . summer.

    (d)| | Spring . . . Winter . . . summer.

41. "How can I give you a match," he asked, <u>when I have my hands full</u>?

    41. (a) || when I have my hands full?

          (b) || "when I have my hands full?"

          (c) || "When I have my hands full?"

          (d) || "when I have my hands full"?

42. <u>"He shouted, They've landed!"</u>

    42. (a) || "He shouted, They've landed!"

          (b) || "He shouted," They've landed!

          (c) || He shouted, "They've landed!"

          (d) || He shouted, "They've landed"!

43. The car struck <u>they</u>.

    43. (a) || they

          (b) || him

          (c) || I

          (d) || he

44. There is the cat <u>who</u> caught the rat.

    44. (a) || who

          (b) || that he

          (c) || that

          (d) || he

45. He tried <u>hardly</u>.

    45. (a) || hardly.

          (b) || harding.

          (c) || harded.

          (d) || hard.

46. <u>My husband a factory worker,</u> is on strike.

    46. (a)| |My husband a factory worker,

       (b)| |My husband, a factory worker,

       (c)| |My husband a factory worker

       (d)| |My husband, a factory worker

47. I am more careful than <u>him</u>.

    47. (a)| |him.

       (b)| |I.

       (c)| |he.

       (d)| |our.

48. The eight bald men drank <u>the coldest soda</u> than the seven fat women did.

    48. (a)| |the coldest soda

       (b)| |cold soda

       (c)| |colder soda

       (d)| |more colder soda

49. The <u>men in fact, know</u> nothing about the strike.

    49. (a)| |men in fact, know

       (b)| |men, in fact, know

       (c)| |men in fact know

       (d)| |men, in fact know

50. The counter will measure six feet long, and the dance floor <u>is</u> no bigger than a dime.

    50. (a)| |is

       (b)| |are

       (c)| |will be

       (d)| |was

51. He put on his new shoes, found his hat, and <u>goes</u> out to get Valerie.

    51. (a)| |goes

       (b)| |had gone

       (c)| |went

       (d)| |is going

52. Everyone brought <u>their</u> own sandwich.

   52. (a)| | their
      (b)| | her
      (c)| | his
      (d)| | our

53. Some things are as plain as <u>people's</u> noses.

   53. (a)| | people's
      (b)| |peoples'
      (c)| | peoples
      (d)| |people

54. <u>When he turned the corner. He saw her.</u>

   54. (a)| | When he turned the corner. He saw her.
      (b)| | When he turned the corner! He saw her.
      (c)| | When he turned the corner, he saw her.
      (d)| | When he turned the corner he saw her.

55. This "improved" instant coffee is <u>more bad</u> than the old one.

   55. (a)| | more bad
      (b)| |worse
      (c)| | badder
      (d)| | bad

56. <u>The dog which was tied to a parking meter. Barked at everyone.</u>

   56. (a)| | The dog which was tied to a parking meter. Barked at everyone.
      (b)| | The dog, which was tied to a parking meter; barked at everyone.
      (c)| | The dog, which was tied to a parking meter, barked at everyone.
      (d)| | The dog, which was tied to a parking meter. Barked at everyone.

57. We looked for hours in the <u>woods but</u>
    we couldn't find the men.

   57. (a) | | woods but

      (b) | | woods, but

      (c) | | woods, for

      (d) | | woods,

58. She lived in <u>Dayton Ohio, at</u> the time.

   58. (a) | | Dayton Ohio, at

      (b) | | Dayton, Ohio at

      (c) | | Dayton, Ohio, at

      (d) | | Dayton Ohio at

59. Before he started work, he went to
    <u>harper school.</u>

   59. (a) | | harper school.

      (b) | | Harper school.

      (c) | | harper School.

      (d) | | Harper School.

Check Your Answers

Next to each correct answer below is the number of the chapter where you will find that answer explained. Put an X next to the answers you got wrong or skipped. Notice the chapter numbers that are next to your wrong answers. These chapters will give you practice in the language skills that you are weak in.

		Chapter in book			Chapter in book
1. (b)	she	3	35. (b)	He	15
2. (b)	picks	9	36. (a)	They're	15
3. (c)	am washing	6	37. (b)	Whose	15
4. (c)	He	9	38. (a)	had had	7
5. (c)	will go	4, 7	39. (b)	I don't know anything.	16
6. (c)	will go	4, 7	40. (c)	spring . . . winter . . . summer.	23
7. (a)	will sneeze.	4	41. (b)	"when I have my hands full?"	22
8. (b)	blew	4, 7	42. (c)	He shouted, "They've landed!"	22
9. (d)	softly	13	43. (b)	him	3
10. (d)	did	4, 7	44. (c)	that	11
11. (b)	am	5	45. (d)	hard.	13
12. (a)	She	5	46. (b)	My husband, a factory worker,	20
13. (c)	will be	5	47. (c)	he.	11
14. (b)	It	3	48. (c)	colder soda	11
15. (b)	is	9	49. (b)	men, in fact, know	20
16. (c)	worked	7	50. (c)	will be	8
17. (d)	It's	15	51. (c)	went	8
18. (b)	doesn't	15	52. (c)	his	14
19. (c)	kind of	17	53. (a)	people's	14
20. (b)	lie down	17	54. (c)	When he turned the corner, he saw her.	24
21. (c)	sure?	18	55. (b)	worse	11
22. (d)	are	9	56. (c)	The dog, which was tied to a parking meter, barked at everyone.	24
23. (a)	wants	9	57. (b)	woods, but	19
24. (c)	looks	9	58. (c)	Dayton, Ohio, at	21
25. (d)	May 19, 1925.	21	59. (d)	Harper School.	23
26. (c)	among	17			
27. (b)	like	9			
28. (a)	milk, and	19			
29. (b)	himself.	10			
30. (c)	I.	10			
31. (d)	he	10			
32. (a)	you and me,	12			
33. (d)	her or me.	12			
34. (b)	can hardly	16			

2. NOUNS

Read the following selection:

Bill Jackson and Harry Monroe lived in the same apartment building in Chicago. On Saturday afternoon each week they met at a bowling alley on Division Street. Bill had his own bowling ball and a new pair of light brown bowling shoes. Harry rented shoes and used one of the balls that belonged to the bowling alley. After both men had thrown a few practice balls, they began the game. As they bowled, Bill teased Harry about the red shoes he had rented and the old, chipped ball he was using. When they finished their game, however, Harry had scored 176 to Bill's total of 137. As Bill handed Harry the dollar they had bet, he said, "Next week I get to wear the red shoes."

In the story above, find the names of two *persons* and write them in

the blanks: _____   _____

Next find the names of two *places* and write them in the blanks:

_____   _____

Now find the names of two *things* and write them in the blanks:

_____   _____

LEARNING
GOALS:
• To identify
  nouns

• To recognize
  singular and
  plural nouns

• To form the
  plural of
  nouns

Bill Jackson and Harry Monroe are the names of two persons. Chicago, Division Street, and bowling alley are the names of places. Ball and shoes are the names of two things. Are there names of other things in the story?

The words that name persons, places, or things are called NOUNS. Any time you give a name to a person, place, or thing, you are using a noun.

What is the name of the person sitting next to you? Where is he from? Is his name a noun? Is the name of the place that he is from a noun?

All the following words are nouns:

worker	train	candy
apple	desk	school
lady	Africa	baby
California	brick	bus
Maria	field	rat

Look around the room you are in. Can you name ten things that are nouns?

Try It

The cast list for the movie *Grease* is given below. Underline the nouns in it.

John Travolta	Olivia Newton-John	Stockard Channing
Eve Arden	Frankie Avalon	Joan Blondell
Edd Byrnes	Sid Caesar	Alice Ghostley
Dody Goodman	Sha Na Na	

Try It Again

Identify each of the nouns below by writing one of these letters in each blank: P if the noun names a person, PL if the noun names a place, or T if the noun names a thing.

_____ticket	_____President	_____car
_____ball	Carter	_____Ohio
_____New York	_____clock	_____doctor
_____Arthur	_____Mexico	_____Reggie Jackson
Ashe	_____teacher	_____Puerto Rico
_____Nigeria	_____airplane	

Try It Again

Pick out the nouns. Tell why you think they are nouns. For example:
sidewalk—a thing.

sidewalk	banana	Anna
chewed	Italy	foreman
union	newspaper	elevator
is	were	yellow
superintendent	soda	bounced
Florida	welfare	hunger
corn	was talking	quickly

NOUNS—SINGULAR AND PLURAL

The noun book is singular. It stands for only one book. The noun books
is plural. It stands for more than one book. When a noun stands for one
person, place, or thing, it is SINGULAR. When it stands for more than
one person, place, or thing, it is PLURAL.

Try It

Put an s after each word below that is a noun and that you could have
more than one of.

pencil	before	these
radio	when	tent
slowly	rabbit	into
picture	if	from

Try It Again

Put an S before the words that are singular and a P before the words
that are plural.

____bottle	____parks	____hot dogs
____chairs	____book	____wheels
____foot	____school	____shoe
____bicycle	____dollar	____warden
____trees	____stores	____girls

As you can see, most nouns are made plural by adding s to the end.
There are other nouns, however, that add es or change their spelling to

show more than one. A few of the common words that add <u>es</u> or change their spelling in the plural are listed below:

Singular	Plural
match	matches
box	boxes
man	men
woman	women
mouse	mice
foot	feet
child	children
tooth	teeth

Try It in a Paragraph

Read the following story. Pick out the noun from the four words taken from each sentence and listed at the right. Blacken the space next to the letter of the noun you choose.

1. On the way home from the bowling alley, Bill and Harry walked through the park.

   1. (a)| | from
   (b)| | park
   (c)| | walked
   (d)| | through

2. They stopped for a few minutes to watch the ducks swimming in the water.

   2. (a)| | stopped
   (b)| | the
   (c)| | swimming
   (d)| | water

3. One duck swam far behind the rest of the ducks.

   3. (a)| | swam
   (b)| | far
   (c)| | behind
   (d)| | ducks

4. After watching it for a little while, Bill saw that the duck's leg had some string wrapped around it.

   4. (a)| | after
   (b)| | Bill
   (c)| | had
   (d)| | around

5. The other end of the string was wound around some sticks and paper.

    5. (a)| | string

       (b)| | was

       (c)| | wound

       (d)| | and

6. Bill and Harry could now see why the duck was having so much trouble.

    6. (a)| | could

       (b)| | why

       (c)| | duck

       (d)| | so

7. They found a long stick and caught the string on it.

    7. (a)| | found

       (b)| | long

       (c)| | stick

       (d)| | caught

8. They pulled the string through the water to the shore.

    8. (a)| | pulled

       (b)| | through

       (c)| | the

       (d)| | shore

9. Then Bill broke the string.

    9. (a)| | Then

       (b)| | Bill

       (c)| | broke

       (d)| | the

10. They both watched the duck swim quickly away to be with the others at the far side of the pond.

    10. (a)| | watched

       (b)| | swim

       (c)| | quickly

       (d)| | pond

3. WORDS THAT REPLACE NOUNS: PRONOUNS

LEARNING GOALS:

• To identify pronouns

• To replace nouns with pronouns that make sense

• To identify singular and plural pronouns

Nouns can be replaced by smaller words like it, she, he they, me, and you. These smaller words are called PRONOUNS. This is how sentences would sound if there were no pronouns:

> Jerry got into the new car that Jerry had just bought.
> As Jerry took the keys from the salesperson, Jerry dropped the keys.

Here are the same sentences with pronouns taking the place of most of the nouns:

> Jerry got into the new car that he had just bought.
> As he took the keys from the salesperson, Jerry dropped them.

In the first sentence, the pronoun he takes the place of the noun Jerry. In the second sentence, he again takes the place of the noun Jerry, and the pronoun them takes the place of the noun keys.

In this chapter you will learn about such pronouns as I, you, he, she, it, him, we, and they. These pronouns are used to take the place of the names of persons, places, or things.

Look at the underlined words in the following story. These words are pronouns. Each one takes the place of a noun.

> Once a young man went to work for the Brown Manufacturing Company as a janitor in the warehouse. It was a dirty place to work, and the pay was low and the hours long. The young man worked hard, however, and never gave up hope that he would some day be a success.
>
> In two months' time Mr. Brown, the owner, decided to make the young man foreman of the plant at three times the pay he had been making.
>
> At the end of six months Mr. Brown called him into his office and told him that he was going to make him treasurer of the company at ten times the salary he had been earning.
>
> At the end of the year Mr. Brown invited the young man to go to a restaurant with him to discuss the young man's promotion to president of Brown Manufacturing.

The young man answered, "I'd like to go to the restaurant with <u>you</u>, Dad, but Mom said <u>she</u> was going to fix supper for <u>us</u>."

Try It

Read the sentences below from the story and choose the words that tell what noun the pronoun is replacing. Blacken the space next to your letter choice.

1. <u>It</u> was a dirty place to work, and the pay was low and the hours long.

   (a)| | the work
   (b)| | the warehouse
   (c)| | the janitor
   (d)| | the company

2. The young man worked hard, however, and never gave up hope that <u>he</u> would some day be a success.

   (a)| | Mr. Brown
   (b)| | the foreman
   (c)| | the young man
   (d)| | the owner

3. In two months' time Mr. Brown, the owner, decided to make the young man foreman of the plant at three times the pay <u>he</u> had been making.

   (a)| | Mr. Brown
   (b)| | the treasurer
   (c)| | the young man
   (d)| | the owner

4. At the end of six months Mr. Brown called <u>him</u> into his office and told <u>him</u> that he was going to make <u>him</u> treasurer of the company at ten times the salary he had been earning.

   (a)| | Mr. Brown
   (b)| | the janitor
   (c)| | the young man
   (d)| | the owner

5. At the end of six months Mr. Brown called him into <u>his</u> office and told him that he was going to make him treasurer of the company at ten times the salary he had been earning.

   (a)| | Mr. Brown
   (b)| | the janitor
   (c)| | the young man
   (d)| | the foreman

6. At the end of six months Mr. Brown called him into his office and told him that <u>he</u> was going to make him treasurer of the company at ten times the salary he had been earning.

(a)|| Mr. Brown
(b)|| the janitor
(c)|| the young man
(d)|| the foreman

7. At the end of six months Mr. Brown called him into his office and told him that he was going to make him treasurer of the company at ten times the salary <u>he</u> had been earning.

(a)|| Mr. Brown
(b)|| the owner
(c)|| the young man
(d)|| the president

8. At the end of the year Mr. Brown invited the young man to go to a restaurant with <u>him</u> to discuss the young man's promotion to president of Brown Manufacturing.

(a)|| Mr. Brown
(b)|| the janitor
(c)|| the young man
(d)|| the foreman

9. The young man answered, "<u>I'd</u> like to go to the restaurant with you, Dad, but Mom said she was going to fix supper for us."

(a)|| Mr. Brown
(b)|| the janitor
(c)|| the owner
(d)|| the young man

10. The young man answered, "I'd like to go to the restaurant with <u>you</u>, Dad, but Mom said she was going to fix supper for us."

(a)|| Mr. Brown
(b)|| the janitor
(c)|| Mom
(d)|| the young man

11. The young man answered, "I'd like to go to the restaurant with you, Dad, but Mom said <u>she</u> was going to fix supper for us."

(a)|| Mr. Brown
(b)|| the young man
(c)|| Mom
(d)|| the foreman

12. The young man answered, "I'd like to go to the restaurant with you, Dad, but Mom said she was going to fix supper for us."

(a)| | Mr. Brown

(b)| | the young man

(c)| | Mr. Brown and the young man

(d)| | Mom and the janitor

Pronouns, like nouns, may be singular or plural. Singular pronouns take the place of nouns that mean <u>one</u> person, place, or thing. Plural pronouns take the place of nouns that mean <u>more than one</u> person, place, or thing. For example:

Singular	Plural
I	we
you	you
he, she, it	they

Try It

Look at the list below and put <u>S</u> next to the pronouns that refer to one person, place, or thing. Put <u>P</u> next to those that refer to more than one. Can any of them be either singular or plural?

____me	____her	____his	____many
____you	____it	____my	____he
____she	____we	____their	____few
____they	____him	____this	____one
____I	____them	____these	____all

Try It Again

Read each sentence below and write in the pronoun that makes the most sense to you. If you have trouble, look at the list of pronouns above.

1. The dogs barked at the old man. _____ turned and shook his cane at them.
2. Mrs. Juarez could not find a new coat for spring. _____ old coat will have to do until next year.
3. Maria and Ann are going to the show tonight. Afterward _____ are going out for pizza.
4. Don't put carrots on Mike's plate. Mike won't eat _____.
5. Joyce likes to baby-sit for the neighbors. _____ would rather do that than watch her own brothers and sisters.

6. When you are finished with the paper, give it to _____.

7. The cut on Al's arm is very deep. I don't think _____ will heal for a long time.

8. When Mr. Fisher and I finish fixing his car, _____ are going to go for a ride to the lake.

9. Billy liked to play baseball with the older children, but the bigger kids would never let _____ bat.

10. The operator will give _____ the number if you dial for information.

Try It in a Paragraph

Read the story below. Decide whether or not the underlined pronouns are used correctly. If the pronoun in a sentence is incorrect, choose the correct pronoun from the choices lettered (a) to (d) on the right-hand side of the page. Blacken the space next to your letter choice. Choice (a) is always the same as the underlined pronoun in the sentence.

1. Janice Moore liked to sleep late in the morning. <u>Her</u> would not get up when her mother called her.

   1. (a)||Her
     (b)||They
     (c)||She
     (d)||He

2. Because Janice stayed in bed so long, she was often late to <u>his</u> school.

   2. (a)||his
     (b)||her
     (c)||she
     (d)||their

3. Janice's teacher warned Janice that <u>she</u> must get to school on time.

   3. (a)||she
     (b)||it
     (c)||her
     (d)||they

4. But Janice would not listen to her mother or to her teacher. She ignored <u>they</u>.

   4. (a)||they
     (b)||her
     (c)||she
     (d)||them

5. Finally Janice's teacher, Mrs. Wilson, told <u>them</u> that if she came to school late again without a note from her mother, she would have to stay after school.

    5. (a)|| them

       (b)|| her

       (c)|| she

       (d)|| they

6. Janice, however, did not listen. The next morning she slept too long and was late for school. As Mrs. Wilson had warned, <u>it</u> kept Janice after school.

    6. (a)|| it

       (b)|| them

       (c)|| she

       (d)|| her

7. The next morning, Janice arrived at school late again, but this time she had a note. She handed <u>they</u> to Mrs. Wilson.

    7. (a)|| they

       (b)|| them

       (c)|| him

       (d)|| it

8. The note said "Janice got up early this morning to go to school, but <u>me</u> caused her to be late. Please don't keep her after school. Sincerely, My Mother."

    8. (a)|| me

       (b)|| it

       (c)|| he

       (d)|| I

4. VERBS TELL WHAT IS HAPPENING

NASA

A. T. & T

Long Island State Park Commission

The word or words that tell what happens in a sentence are called VERBS. Verbs tell what someone or something does. Some verbs show action. Run, fall, drive, hit, and kick are verbs that show action.

Look at the sentences below. What words tell what someone or something does?

> Bill ran on the beach.
> Carla talked on the phone.
> The horses walked.
> The druggist poured the medicine.

The words that show action are ran, talked, walked, and poured.

Sometimes you cannot see the action that is taking place, as in such verbs as think, hope, and see. Even though you can't see the action, these verbs are still called action verbs.

24

Try It

Underline the word in each sentence that shows action.

1. Mrs. Brown went to the post office.
2. Mr. Bailey painted the mailbox yellow.
3. Sandra likes peanut-butter sandwiches.
4. The glass smashed on the floor.
5. Jan baked a cake for the family.
6. The old woman slipped on the icy steps.
7. Jesse watched the game on TV.
8. The two men fought each other in the alley.
9. Keith rode his bicycle to work.
10. Mrs. McGee sold the old dishes to her neighbor.

Try It Again

Underline the words in the news item that show action.

Pirates 3, Expos 1
PITTSBURGH, July 4 (AP)—Bert Blyleven rapped a three-run double and scattered five hits over eight innings to lead the Pittsburgh Pirates to a 3-1 victory over the Montreal Expos today in the first game of a doubleheader.

Besides telling what happens, verbs tell you when it happens. Verbs tell you if something is happening right now (PRESENT TENSE), if something has already happened (PAST TENSE), or if something is going to happen (FUTURE TENSE). Look at the verb call. Notice how it changes from present to past to future tense.

Present Tense

Singular	Plural
I call	we call
you call	you call
he ⎫	
she ⎬ calls	they call
it ⎭	

Past Tense

I called	we called
you called	you called
he	
she } called	they called
it	

Future Tense

I shall call	we shall call
you will call	you will call
he	
she } will call	they will call
it	

Notice that the verb has an s added in the present tense when it goes with he, she, or it. The past tense will often have ed added to the verb. The future tense always has the word will or shall in front of the verb.

Try It

Put each of the verbs below in one of the sentences that follow. In each sentence, use the verb that makes the most sense.

dusted	rode
snowed	opened
found	honked
laughed	started
bit	arrested

1. Fred _____ the horse.

2. It _____ yesterday.

3. Gloria _____ the window.

4. The dog _____ the mailman.

5. The bus driver _____ the horn.

6. The policeman _____ the pusher.

7. Joyce _____ at Mel's joke.

8. Cal _____ the furniture.

9. Sue _____ the motorcycle in the garage.

10. We _____ the purse under the chair.

When did the action take place in each of the ten sentences you just completed? Did the action happen in the present, past, or future? If you said past, you are correct. How did you know the sentences were written in the past tense?

Try It Again

Listed below are three columns. The second column is a list of verbs in the past tense. In the first column, write the present tense of the verb. In the third column, write the future tense.

Present	Past	Future
1. _____	1. rode	1. _____
2. _____	2. snowed	2. _____
3. _____	3. opened	3. _____
4. _____	4. bit	4. _____
5. _____	5. honked	5. _____
6. _____	6. arrested	6. _____
7. _____	7. laughed	7. _____
8. _____	8. dusted	8. _____
9. _____	9. started	9. _____
10. _____	10. found	10. _____

Try It Again

Read the sentences below and underline the words (verbs) that tell what happens. At the end of each sentence, write *present*, *past*, or *future* to tell when the action takes place.

1. I will go to the movie with you. _____
2. Our team lost two softball games last year. _____
3. Mary needs new shoes for school. _____
4. Who will buy that junk in the alley? _____
5. Jeff searched under the house with a flashlight. _____
6. We will miss Jake this summer. _____
7. Harriet said good-bye to us. _____
8. The doctor came to the accident right away. _____
9. Please open the door. _____
10. They will tear the building down next year. _____

Try It in a Paragraph

Read the story on pages 28-29. Decide whether or not each underlined verb shows that the action is happening *in the present*. If it doesn't, choose the correct verb that shows the present tense from the choices lettered (a) to (d) on the right. Blacken the space next to your letter choice. Choice (a) is always the same as the verb form in the story.

In a small town a man <u>calls</u>[1] the telephone operator every morning.

He <u>asked</u>[2] him for the correct time.

After several weeks the operator <u>became</u>[3] curious.

"Why," he <u>says</u>,[4] "do you <u>called</u>[5] me every morning to ask the time?"

"I <u>have</u>[6] to be very careful about the right time," he explains. "I <u>will blow</u>[7] the noon whistle at the factory."

1. (a)| | calls
   (b)| | called
   (c)| | call
   (d)| | will call

2. (a)| | asked
   (b)| | ask
   (c)| | asks
   (d)| | asking

3. (a)| | became
   (b)| | become
   (c)| | becomes
   (d)| | will become

4. (a)| | says
   (b)| | say
   (c)| | said
   (d)| | saids

5. (a)| | called
   (b)| | calls
   (c)| | call
   (d)| | will call

6. (a)| | have
   (b)| | has
   (c)| | haves
   (d)| | will have

7. (a)| | will blow
   (b)| | blew
   (c)| | blow
   (d)| | blows

"Now that <u>is</u>⁸ interesting to hear," the operator <u>will answer</u>⁹.

8. (a)| | is

(b)| | was

(c)| | will be

(d)| | were

9. (a)| | will answer.

(b)| | answer.

(c)| | answered.

(d)| | answers.

"Every day at noon I <u>set</u>¹⁰ our clock by your whistle."

10. (a)| | set

(b)| | sit

(c)| | sets

(d)| | sits

5. THE VERB "BE"

LEARNING GOALS:

• To identify the present, past, and future tenses of **be**

• To learn when to use **is, are, am, was, were, and will be**

The word **be** is a verb, but often it doesn't seem like a verb. **Be** doesn't show action or movement. Like other verbs, however, it has more than one form. Here are the forms of **be** in the present tense:

Singular	Plural
I am	we are
you are	you are
he ⎫	they are
she ⎬ is	
it ⎭	

These forms of the verb **be** connect the thing talked about in a sentence with a word or words that tell something about that thing. For example, look at this sentence:

He is happy.

The thing talked about is he. The word that tells something about he is happy. The word is (a form of be) links he and happy together.

As you can see, the forms of **be** that are used in the present tense are **am, is,** and **are. Am** is used only with **I.**

I am happy.

Is is used with the pronouns **he, she,** and **it** and with nouns that can be replaced by he, she or it.

He is happy.
Jim is happy.
Beverly is happy.
It is happy.
The cat is happy.

Are is used with **they, you,** and **we** and with nouns that can be replaced by they, you, and we.

They are happy.
The women are happy.
You are happy.
We are happy.
The girls and I are happy.

Try It

Put is, are, or am in each blank in the following sentences.

1. I _____ happy.
2. Richard _____ sad.
3. The radiators _____ hot.
4. The teen-agers _____ excited about the record.
5. We _____ angry because they didn't finish their work.
6. The dog _____ sleepy.
7. Cigarettes _____ harmful to your health.
8. The water _____ dirty.
9. The coffee _____ too hot to drink.
10. It _____ delicious!

Now look at these sentences:

He was happy last week.
They were happy yesterday.

Was and were are other forms of be. What tense are was and were?
You can tell from the words yesterday and last week in these sentences that these forms of be are in the past tense.
Here are the forms of be in the past tense:

I was	we were
you were	you were
he was	they were
she was	
it was	

Two forms of the verb be end with s. They are is and was. These forms follow the pronouns he, she, and it. They also follow the nouns that these pronouns replace. Here are some examples:

The pot was dirty yesterday.
It was dirty.
It is dirty.

Gordon was angry.
He was angry yesterday afternoon.
He is angry.
The woman is happy.
She is happy.
She was happy this morning.

If you aren't sure whether was or is should follow a noun, ask yourself whether the noun can be replaced by he, she, or it. If it can, you know was or is can follow the noun.

Was is also used to show past action for the pronoun I.

I was here.
I was as angry as Gordon.

Were is always used with the pronouns you, we, and they and always shows past action. For example, look at this sentence:

John and I were happy last night.

The pronoun we can take the place of John and I:

We were happy last night.

Try It

Put was or were in each blank. Remember that these forms of be show past action.

1. Sally _____ happy.
2. The puppy _____ happy.
3. Joe and Pete _____ happy.
4. I _____ happy.
5. The men _____ happy.
6. Ann and her husband _____ happy.
7. Alice and I _____ happy.
8. We _____ happy.
9. He _____ happy.
10. You _____ happy.

Now read this joke:

"How long did it take your son to learn how to drive a car?"
"It will be ten years in September."

When <u>will</u> and <u>be</u> are next to each other they show the future tense.

> I will be there in a minute.
> He will be happy when he sees you washed his car.

Here are the forms of <u>be</u> as it is used in the future tense.

I will be	we will be
you will be	you will be
he will be	they will be
she will be	
it will be	

Try It

Put the correct form of <u>be</u> in the blank space in each sentence below. If there are no other words in the sentence like <u>yesterday</u> or <u>next week</u> that help you know when the action happened, use the present tense of the verb.

1. He _____ arrested yesterday.
2. She _____ sure the bail is too high.
3. They _____ on their way to the meeting when it happened.
4. We _____ there about noon if the car holds out that long.
5. The package _____ here tomorrow.
6. You _____ silly.
7. He _____ my husband.
8. I _____ alone when I heard footsteps in the hall.
9. Yes, I _____ mad at you.
10. It _____ raining now.

Try It in a Paragraph

Read the story below. Then read it again and decide whether or not each underlined verb is used correctly. If a verb is not correct, choose the correct verb from the choices lettered (a) to (d) on the right. Blacken the space next to the letter choice you make. Choice (a) is always the same as the underlined verb in the story.

               1   2

Two men <u>were</u> traveling on a train. One <u>were</u> busy

1. (a) | | were

   (b) | | was

   (c) | | is

   (d) | | be

reading his newspaper. The other is³ looking out the window. After a while, the first man asked the second for a match to light his pipe. In a few minutes they is⁴ talking.

2. (a)| | were

   (b)| | was

   (c)| | be

   (d)| | are

3. (a)| | is

   (b)| | was

   (c)| | were

   (d)| | be

4. (a)| | is

   (b)| | was

   (c)| | were

   (d)| | am

"When do you think we will been⁵ in Kalamazoo?" the first asked.

5. (a)| | will been

   (b)| | be

   (c)| | wills be

   (d)| | will be

"Oh, is⁶ you going to Kalamazoo, too?" the other replied.

6. (a)| | is

   (b)| | was

   (c)| | are

   (d)| | will

"We is⁷ supposed to arrive there at 8 o'clock."

7. (a)| | is

   (b)| | was

   (c)| | will be

   (d)| | are

8
"What is your line of work?" asked the first.

8. (a)| | is

(b)| | are

(c)| | were

(d)| | be

9
The second man said, "I is a construction worker."

9. (a)| | is

(b)| | am

(c)| | are

(d)| | be

The first man threw out his hand. "Shake," he said.
10
"So be I."

10. (a)| | be

(b)| | is

(c)| | am

(d)| | are

6. MORE ABOUT THE PRESENT

New York Convention and Visitors Bureau

NASA

LEARNING GOALS:

- **To find out two ways of forming the present tense**

- **To learn how to show that something is happening right now**

- **To learn how to show that something happens often**

Verbs can show that something is happening in the present in two ways:
1. Verbs can show that something happens often, all the time, or regularly in the present even though it may not be happening right now.

> People row boats on the lake in Central Park.
> Halley's comet appears every seventy-five years.

In each sentence, the verb tells that something happens regularly or often even if it isn't happening right now.
2. Verbs can also show that something is happening right now.

Look carefully at this telephone conversation. The verbs that show something happening right now in the present are underlined.

> "Hello? Yes, this is Juan. No, I was in the shower. Yeah, I'm standing here in a puddle of water that is getting bigger and wetter every second. Talk louder. I can't hear you. The water in the shower is still running. Who? Rita? No, you have the wrong number."

In this paragraph you know that Juan is talking on the telephone now.

You learned about verbs that show present action on page 24. Remember that the verb is spelled the same way each time it is used, except when it follows the pronouns he, she, and it, or the nouns they can stand for. Then the verb ends in s.

She wears a blue coat.

The following sentences have verbs that show something is happening right now:

I am painting my refrigerator red.
He is shouting at his dog.
They are eating their left-over dinner for breakfast.

Each verb begins with am, are, or is. Each verb also has the special ending -ing.

Try It

Circle the verbs that show something is happening right now.

1. running
2. is running
3. take
4. are taking
5. took

6. am eating
7. is drinking
8. drinking
9. drank
10. am dancing

Try It Again

In front of each sentence below is a verb in parentheses. Change each of those verbs to make it show something is happening right now and put it in the blank.

(chew)   1. She _____ gum.
(protect)   2. The dog _____ the apartment.
(enjoy)   3. They _____ the movie.
(walk)   4. I _____ the dog.
(drink)   5. He _____ a bottle of root beer.

Try It Again

Some of the sentences below show that something is happening right now. Others show that something happens regularly or often. Put the correct form of the verb in parentheses in each sentence below.

1. When you (think) _____ it might rain, take your umbrella. It's sure not to.

2. Right now, they (watch) _____ the election returns on television.

3. He often (go) _____ to a restaurant where he gets all he can eat for $1.59.

4. She usually (travel) _____ home by subway.

5. The cat (lick) _____ his paws after he eats.

6. John, do you know that you (wear) _____ two different kinds of socks?

7. She (sleep) _____ late every morning.

8. He usually (miss) _____ the bus.

9. What am I doing? I (wash) _____ the dishes. Do you want to help dry them?

10. My shoes (need) _____ new heels.

Try It in a Paragraph

Read the story below. Decide whether or not each underlined verb shows something is happening right now. If it does not, change it so it does show something is happening right now. Choose the correct verb form from the choices lettered (a) to (d). Blacken the space next to your letter choice. Choice (a) is always the same as the verb form in the story.

1. A man is <u>walking</u> along a road.

   1. (a)| | is walking

      (b)| | are walking

      (c)| | walk

      (d)| | walks

2. He sees a crowd of boys who <u>sit</u> in a circle with a small dog.

   2. (a)| | sit

      (b)| | sits

      (c)| | are sitting

      (d)| | is sitting

3. The dog <u>walk</u> around in the center.

   3. (a)| | walk

      (b)| | is walking

      (c)| | walks

      (d)| | walked

4. "What <u>are you doing</u> with that dog?" he asks.

   4. (a)| | are you doing

      (b)| | is you doing

      (c)| | do you do

      (d)| | did you do

5. "We <u>is telling</u> lies," one of the boys says. "Whoever tells the biggest lie wins the dog."

   5. (a)| | is telling

      (b)| | are telling

      (c)| | tell

      (d)| | tells

6. "Oh," <u>says</u> the man. "I am surprised at you boys. When I was young like you I never told a lie."

   6. (a)| | says

      (b)| | say

      (c)| | said

      (d)| | saying

7. There <u>was</u> a moment of silence. Then one of the boys says, "Give the man the dog, Jim."

   7. (a)| | was

      (b)| | is

      (c)| | are

      (d)| | were

7. HELPING VERBS

LEARNING GOALS:

- **To find out how to use helping verbs like have, has, had, can, could, would, should, and must**

- **To learn the past and past with have/has of some irregular verbs**

- **To recognize divided verbs**

You have seen that a verb may be a single word such as <u>ran</u>, <u>needs</u>, <u>lost</u>, and <u>came</u> or that a verb may be made up of more than one word such as <u>will go</u>, <u>is running</u>, <u>will buy</u>, and <u>are taking</u>. Many verbs that you see and use are more than one word. Look at these three sentences:

> George <u>has gone</u> to the beach.
> Bertha <u>could lift</u> the chair by herself.
> The clock <u>has been broken</u> for a week.

When a verb is made up of two or more words, the last word is called the MAIN VERB. The words that come before it are called HELPING VERBS. In the three sentences above, the main verbs are <u>gone</u>, <u>lift</u>, and <u>broken</u>. The helping verbs are <u>has</u>, <u>could</u>, and <u>has been</u>. All the words listed below may be used as helping verbs:

be	have	may
is	had	might
are	can	shall
was	could	do
were	would	does
am	should	did
been	must	
has	will	

HAS, HAVE, AND HAD

You have seen in Chapter 5 how the verb <u>be</u> can be used. Now look carefully at the ways <u>have</u> and <u>has</u> are used in these pairs of sentences:

> I <u>have</u> pens, pencils, and paper.
> He <u>has</u> old shoes, faded pants, and stained ties.

> I <u>have worked</u> in this factory for twenty-five years.
> He <u>has worn</u> two different shirts for as long as I can remember.

In the first two sentences, <u>have</u> and <u>has</u> are the verbs. They show that the things belong to the people in the sentences. The action in these sentences is in the present.

But in the last two sentences, the words have and has are helping verbs that help the main verb show that something has happened. Have worked is one verb made up of two words. Has worn is also one verb made up of two words. In these verbs, have and has do not show possession or belonging.

What is the difference in meaning between these two sentences?

> He worked in this factory for twenty-five years.
> He has worked in this factory for twenty-five years.

Both sentences tell of something that happened in the past. But the first sentence means that he worked there for twenty-five years and stopped. The second sentence means that he worked there for twenty-five years and is still working there.

Has or have before a verb means the thing that is happening started in the past and is still going on in the present. In the sentence "She has always combed her hair before breakfast," the verb has combed means she still combs her hair every morning before breakfast. The verb that follows have or has usually has -ed added to the end of it.

Try It

Circle the verbs that show that something started in the past and is still going on in the present.

has walked   have tripped
limped   stumbled
had scuffled   has staggered
is hobbling   crawled
creep

IRREGULAR VERBS

Some verbs do not end in -ed when they follow has or have. These verbs change their spelling when they show that something started in the past and is still going on. They also change their spelling when they show that the thing that happened in the past also stopped in the past. Here is a list of some of these verbs. They are called IRREGULAR VERBS.

Present	Past	Past with have/has
I swim	I swam	I have swum He has swum
I begin	I began	I have begun He has begun

Present	Past	Past with have/has
I ring	I rang	I have rung He has rung
I drive	I drove	I have driven He has driven
I ride	I rode	I have ridden He has ridden
I write	I wrote	I have written He has written
I take	I took	I have taken He has taken
I break	I broke	I have broken He has broken
I freeze	I froze	I have frozen He has frozen
I speak	I spoke	I have spoken He has spoken
I steal	I stole	I have stolen He has stolen
I swear	I swore	I have sworn He has sworn
I tear	I tore	I have torn He has torn
I wear	I wore	I have worn He has worn
I teach	I taught	I have taught He has taught
I give	I gave	I have given He has given
I catch	I caught	I have caught He has caught
I come	I came	I have come He has come

Present	Past	Past with have/has
I run	I ran	I have run He has run
I sit	I sat	I have sat He has sat
I eat	I ate	I have eaten He has eaten
I blow	I blew	I have blown He has blown
I draw	I drew	I have drawn He has drawn
I fall	I fell	I have fallen He has fallen
I grow	I grew	I have grown He has grown
I know	I knew	I have known He has known
I throw	I threw	I have thrown He has thrown
I leave	I left	I have left He has left

The following three verbs are often hard to remember to use correctly. Think twice when you use them.

Present	Past	Past with have/has
I go	I went	I have gone He has gone
I do	I did	I have done He has done
I see	I saw	I have seen He has seen

These spelling changes must be learned by heart. A good way to learn is by using them often.

WHEN DO YOU USE <u>HAS</u> AND <u>HAVE</u>?

Has ends in <u>s</u> like <u>is</u>, <u>smells</u>, and <u>sleeps</u>. The <u>s</u> at the end of a verb means that the verb follows the pronouns <u>it</u>, <u>she</u>, and <u>he</u>. Remember that these pronouns take the place of singular nouns such as <u>the car</u>, <u>Alice</u>, and <u>the man</u>.

> She (Alice) <u>has given</u> birth to two sets of twins
> in two years.

Have is used with plural nouns and with pronouns such as <u>we</u> and <u>they</u> that replace those nouns. <u>Have</u> is also used with <u>I</u> and <u>you</u>.

> We <u>have borrowed</u> money from a bank.
> I <u>have cashed</u> my check.
> You <u>have answered</u> my question.

Try It

In each sentence below, fill the blank with <u>have</u> or <u>has</u> and the correct form of the verb that is in parentheses.

1. You don't know how hard I (work) _____ these last few weeks.

2. He (use) _____ that same excuse ever since he could talk.

3. From that day on, I (try) _____ to behave myself.

4. For five years, he (go) _____ to the farmer's market every morning at 5 A.M.

5. I (see) _____ never _____ anyone who could put something over on that woman. [<u>Never</u> separates the two words in the verb.]

6. That dog (walk) _____ always _____ a little sideways; you don't know whether it's going or coming.

7. He (do) _____ more favors for me than anyone else.

8. Truck drivers (stop) _____ and (eat) _____ at Joe's Diner for years.

9. Those two brothers (make) _____ good money ever since they came to this country.

10. For two months now, you (sit) _____ in that same chair every day.

WHEN DO YOU USE <u>HAD</u>?

You have learned that the verbs <u>have</u> and <u>has</u> can be used in two ways. Another verb that can be used two ways is <u>had</u>.
1. <u>Had</u> can show belonging.
2. <u>Had</u> can also help the main verb show something that has already happened.

Watch how <u>had</u> is used in the following sentences:

> I <u>had</u> a snake in my bathtub.
> You <u>had</u> a funny idea.
> Before I understood your idea, you <u>had run</u> into
>   the yard.
> You left the hospital after you <u>had recovered</u>.

The action in all four sentences happened in the past. The last two sentences have two verbs in them. The verb with <u>had</u> in it shows the action happened and was finished in the past.

A verb is spelled the same way whether it follows <u>had</u>, <u>has</u>, or <u>have</u>. Most of these verbs end in <u>-ed</u>.

> I have walked
> he has walked
> he had walked

The word <u>had</u> may be used with all nouns and pronouns and does not change.

> I had run
> he, she, it had run
> we had run

Try It

Circle the verbs that show an action that has already happened. (These verbs are all different ways of saying "see.")

had looked	had seen
glances	stare
will observe	had peeked
had watched	is gazing

Try It Again

Fill each blank with the correct form of the verb in parentheses. Add <u>had</u> where necessary.

1. I (lock) _____ the car before I remembered the key was inside.
2. He saw only half the worm after he (take) _____ a bite of the apple.
3. She read the salt label after she (pour) _____ half a cup in the cake batter.
4. After she had worked hard all week, she (deserve) _____ a Saturday night out.
5. After they (dance) _____ three numbers in a row, they ordered another pizza.
6. We had tried, but we (fail) _____.
7. What (do) _____ you _____ before the money arrived?
8. The phone (stop) _____ ringing before the man taking a shower reached it.
9. The car (hit) _____ a telephone pole before I (know)_____ what was happening.
10. She (open) _____ the door before she (ask)_____ who it was.

BE PLUS HAS, HAVE, OR HAD

Has, have, and had also help the verb be show something that has already happened. The form of be that is used with these helping words is been.

> I have been a widow for five years.
> He has been studying hard.
> They had been students before they became
> teachers.

Try It

In each sentence below, write has, have, or had before been in the blank space.

1. We _____ been going together for two years now.
2. He _____ been there for twenty-five years before they laid him off.
3. The car _____ been working before we loaned it to you.
4. After he _____ been there a while, he began to win a few games.
5. Where _____ you been? (You can see that you separates the two words in the verb.)
6. We _____ been worried about you.

7. Jesse _____ been looking for a job for weeks.

8. The car engine _____ been making that funny sound for days now.

9. I _____ been sleepy before I drank a cup of coffee.

10. I don't understand how he got lost. He _____ been driving that route for months now.

CAN, COULD, WOULD, SHOULD, AND MUST

There are other words that "help" verbs. They are can, could, would, should, and must. See how they are used in the sentences below. Notice that two words make up one verb as when have, has, and had are used.

> I can dance.
> You could try.
> They would like some, too.
> We should stop at the supermarket.
> He must file his income tax.

Try It

Underline the verbs in the sentences below.

1. He can fix your flat tire.
2. You should try some of her homemade soup.
3. She would dance only at parties.
4. They must move from their apartment.
5. Well, I could ask her tomorrow.

DIVIDED VERBS

Sometimes the two words that make up a verb are separated by other words. Here are some examples. The verb in each sentence is underlined.

> We can never thank you enough.
> The pitcher could certainly throw fast balls.

Words like never and certainly can be moved around in the sentence. They don't have to divide the two words that make up the verb. Try moving the words to other places in the sentences. This will make it easier to see what words make up the verb in each sentence.

Here are examples. The sentences are the same as the ones above, except that the one word that divided the verb has been moved.

We <u>never</u> can thank you enough.
The <u>pitcher</u> <u>certainly</u> could throw fast balls.

Try It

Underline the two words that make up the verb in the following sentences.

1. Where have you been?
2. I have never met her.
3. She would only dance at parties.
4. They must soon move from their apartment.
5. You should really try some of her homemade soup.

Try It in a Paragraph

Read the story below and decide whether or not each underlined word is used correctly. If a word is not used correctly, choose the correct word from the choices lettered (a) to (d) on the right. Blacken the space next to your letter choice. Choice (a) is always the same as the word in the story.

1. Early one morning a man stopped his car outside a diner. Before the waiter <u>has</u> a chance to open the blinds,

   1. (a) || has
      (b) || have
      (c) || had
      (d) || wants

2. the man <u>had rushed</u> inside. After his

   2. (a) || had rushed
      (b) || has rushed
      (c) || have rushed
      (d) || rushed

3. eyes <u>have finally got</u> used to the dark,

   3. (a) || have finally got
      (b) || has gotten
      (c) || had finally gotten
      (d) || had finally got

4. he <u>sees</u> the waiter wiping off the bar. The man went up to him and asked whether he knew anything that would stop hiccups.

4. (a)| | sees

   (b)| | saw

   (c)| | see

   (d)| | had seen

5. Before the man <u>had</u> a chance to say anything else, the waiter had slapped him across the face with a wet towel.

5. (a)| | had

   (b)| | have

   (c)| | has

   (d)| | had got

6. The man was surprised and angry. He <u>had demanded</u>

6. (a)| | had demanded

   (b)| | demands

   (c)| | demanded

   (d)| | has demanded

7. to know why the waiter <u>slaps</u> him.

7. (a)| | slaps

   (b)| | slapped

   (c)| | had slapped

   (d)| | has slapped

8. The waiter smiled and said, "Well, you <u>hasn't</u> any hiccups now, have you?"

8. (a)| | hasn't

   (b)| | hadn't

   (c)| | doesn't have

   (d)| | haven't

9. "I never did <u>has</u>," the man answered. "I wanted something for my wife. She's out in the car."

9. (a)| | has

   (b)| | had

   (c)| | have

   (d)| | do

8. SHIFTING THE "TIME" OF VERBS

LEARNING GOALS:

• **To be able to change the tenses of verbs**

A verb can be written or can be changed in many ways. The verb bite, for example, can change in the following ways:

The dog is biting the man.
The dog bites every man he sees.
The dog bit the man.
The dog will bite the man.
The dog has bitten every man on the block.
The man had bitten the dog before the dog bit the man.

Each different form of the verb bite shows when the action takes place.

When you write a sentence that uses more than one verb, you must be sure you use forms of the verbs that go together and make sense. Look at this sentence:

Don Patterson will take out a match and is lighting his pipe.

This sentence doesn't make sense because you can't tell when the action takes place. The verb will take is in the future tense—it shows action that will take place in the future. But the verb is lighting is in the present tense—it shows action that is taking place right now, in the present. You can't tell when Don Patterson lights his pipe. Will he do it in a minute? Or is he doing it right now? The sentence should read:

Don Patterson will take out a match and will light his pipe.

You can tell from that sentence that the action will take place in the future.

Again, if a sentence has two or more verbs, be sure they make sense together.

Try It

Change the verbs in parentheses in the sentences below so that they show action happening at the same time as the first verb.

50

1. He put on his new shoes, (find) _____ his hat, and (go) _____ out to get Valerie.

2. Every Saturday night, people packed into the club and (dance) _____ until 4 A.M.

3. The counter will measure six feet long, and the dance floor (be) _____ no bigger than a dime.

4. A fat little man is playing the piano, and a young boy (beat) _____ the drums.

5. Slim and Valerie dance and (talk) _____ at the club every Saturday night.

6. The waiter poured a small glass of milk, (hand) _____ it to Valerie, and (collect) _____ thirty cents.

Try It in a Paragraph

A hearse is a long, black car that carries a coffin to a cemetery. Read this story about a hearse and decide whether or not each underlined verb shows action that happened in the past. If a verb does not show past action, choose the correct verb from the four possible answers lettered (a) to (d) at the right-hand side of the page. Blacken the space next to your letter choice. Choice (a) is always the same as the underlined verb in the story.

The driver of a hearse drove up a hilly street. As the hearse reached the top of the street, the driver hears¹ the siren of a fire engine behind him.

1. (a)| | hears
   (b)| | heard
   (c)| | is hearing
   (d)| | had heard

He pulled² the hearse closer to the parked cars. As he did so, the hearse bumps³ into one of the cars.

2. (a)| | pulled
   (b)| | is pulling
   (c)| | pulls
   (d)| | had pulled

3. (a)| | bumps
   (b)| | has bumped
   (c)| | is bumping
   (d)| | bumped

The back door of the hearse <u>had flew</u>⁴ open. The coffin inside the hearse was on a little wagon with wheels.

Before the driver <u>knows</u>⁵ what was happening, the coffin rolled out the back door of the hearse. It <u>rolled</u>⁶ down the hilly street.

People stood on the sidewalk and <u>point</u>⁷ their fingers at the coffin. They couldn't believe what they saw.

The coffin <u>reaches</u>⁸ the bottom of the street and jumped the curb. It sped toward the door of a drug-store.

Just at that moment, a man <u>opens</u>⁹ the door of the drug-store and <u>walked</u>¹⁰ out.

4. (a)| | had flew
   (b)| | is flying
   (c)| | flew
   (d)| | flies

5. (a)| | knows
   (b)| | knew
   (c)| | had known
   (d)| | know

6. (a)| | rolled
   (b)| | is rolling
   (c)| | will roll
   (d)| | rolls

7. (a)| | point
   (b)| | pointed
   (c)| | are pointing
   (d)| | is pointing

8. (a)| | reaches
   (b)| | reached
   (c)| | reach
   (d)| | reaching

9. (a)| | opens
   (b)| | will open
   (c)| | opened
   (d)| | open

10. (a)| | walked

    (b)| | walks

    (c)| | are walking

    (d)| | is walking

The coffin rolled through the open door. It is banging^11

against the drugstore counter, and the lid of the coffin

flew open. As the druggist leaned over the counter, a

little voice from the coffin says,^12 "Do you have anything

to stop this coughin'?"

11. (a)| | is banging

    (b)| | bangs

    (c)| | bang

    (d)| | banged

12. (a)| | says

    (b)| | say

    (c)| | said

    (d)| | will say

CHECKUP TEST 1

LEARNING GOALS:

• To review Chapters 1-8

Nouns

1. Underline the nouns in the list below. Write S in the blank if a noun is singular, P if a noun is plural.

    a. _____ player
    b. _____ racket
    c. _____ balls
    d. _____ hears
    e. _____ sneakers

2. Identify the nouns below by writing P in the blank if a noun names a person, Pl if it names a place, or T if it names a thing.

    a. _____ Alan Aarons
    b. _____ Bourbon Street
    c. _____ New Orleans
    d. _____ helicopter
    e. _____ waiter

3. Underline the nouns in the sentences below.

    a. Janet picked up a pencil.
    b. She took paper from the desk.
    c. She wrote a letter to her mother.
    d. Mrs. Taylor lives in Canada.
    e. She likes to get letters from her daughter.

Pronouns

4. Underline the pronouns in the list below.

    a. Betty
    b. she
    c. I
    d. you
    e. no

5. Find a pronoun in the column at the left that could replace each of the words or group of words at the right. Write the pronoun in the blank next to the word.

we	a. _____	Mr. Black
they	b. _____	Milt and Dan
he	c. _____	Vera and I
she	d. _____	baseball
it	e. _____	Vera

6. Write S next to the singular pronouns and P next to the plural pronouns.

a. _____ him
b. _____ their
c. _____ one
d. _____ its
e. _____ we

Verbs

7. In each sentence, underline the word that shows action.

a. Marcy went to the movies yesterday.
b. She saw a good show.
c. Lew helped Eddie in his job.
d. Andy loves pizza.
e. Carla plays tennis well.

8. Indicate the tense of the following verbs by writing $\underline{P}$ in the blank if they are in the present, $\underline{Pa}$ if they are in the past, and $\overline{F}$ if they are in the future.

a. _____ go
b. _____ rained
c. _____ tried
d. _____ will happen
e. _____ starts

9. The first column below shows the present tense of five verbs. Write the past tense in the second column and the future tense in the third column.

Present	Past	Future
a. I like	a. I _____	a. I _____
b. I join	b. I _____	b. I _____
c. I have	c. I _____	c. I _____
d. I show	d. I _____	d. I _____
e. I do	e. I _____	e. I _____

The Verb "Be"

10. Choose a verb from the column on the left to go with each word or group of words on the right. Write the verb in the blank beside the word. (Some verbs may be used more than once.)

am   a. he _____
is   b. you _____

are   c. I _____
                        d. red, blue, and yellow _____
                        e. it _____

11. Underline the verb in parentheses that should be used in each of the following sentences.

    a. John and Richard (was, were) pleased with the results.
    b. Don (was, were) not.
    c. Helen and I (was, were) going to help you.
    d. You (was, were) my best friend.
    e. She (was, were) Betty's niece.

12. Put the correct form of be in the blank in each sentence below.

    a. You _____ working in an office the last time I saw you.
    b. Tomorrow Saray _____ twenty-one.
    c. Today _____ a holiday.
    d. This _____ the last time I am telling you.
    e. Martin _____ at Rick's house last night.

More about the Present

13. Change each verb to make it show that something is happening in the present. Write the correct verb in the blank.

    a. (love) I _____ you.
    b. (wear) He always _____ his blue tie with that shirt.
    c. (eat) They _____ dinner at seven.
    d. (swim) Maria _____ well.
    e. (go) Terry _____ to the movies alone.

14. In the blanks, rewrite the underlined verbs from the following paragraph so that they show something is happening in the present.

    > The ball <u>sailed</u> into right field and the runners <u>wound</u> up at third and second. Rich Gossage <u>replaced</u> Gullett at that point and <u>induced</u> Jim Sundberg to ground to Bucky Dent, who <u>threw</u> Bonds out at the plate.

    a. _____ sailed
    b. _____ wound
    c. _____ replaced
    d. _____ induced
    e. _____ threw

15. In each sentence, write the correct form of the verb in the blank.

    a. (like) I always _____ dessert.
    b. (go) They _____ to the theater at night.
    c. (leave) Sam usually _____ for work before eight.

d. (do) He _____ it every day.
e. (miss) You often _____ your train.

Helping Verbs

16. Underline the correct verb in each sentence.

   a. I (has, have) never worked.
   b. He (has, have) always been alone.
   c. They (has, have) tried to do their best.
   d. You (has, have) always liked noodles.
   e. Eloise (has, have) been a teacher.

17. Write the past with <u>have/has</u> of these irregular verbs.

   a. I ring   I have _____
   b. I write   I have _____
   c. I take   I have _____
   d. I speak   I have _____
   e. I teach   I have _____

18. Underline the two words that make up the verb in each sentence.

   a. He has never been out of the country.
   b. Mary can hardly run at all.
   c. I am soon going.
   d. Mike has always said so.
   e. You should certainly apply for that job.

Shifting the "Time" of Verbs

19. From the column on the left, choose the verb that is the present tense of one of the verbs on the right. Write the verb you choose in the blank next to the matching verb.

   pause   a. _____ said
   come   b. _____ had
   says   c. _____ came
   has   d. _____ will pause
   is calling   e. _____ called

20. Change the time of each underlined verb so that the sentence makes sense.

   a. When you go, I <u>have followed</u> _____ you.
   b. Hear no evil, <u>saw</u> _____ no evil.
   c. The cat <u>run</u> _____ away yesterday.
   d. Please <u>gave</u> _____ the man a quarter.
   e. It <u>are</u> _____ none of your business.

9. MATCHING NOUNS AND VERBS

Selda Scharlin from Monkmeyer Press Photo Service

Louise Van Der Meid from Monkmeyer Press Photo Service

LEARNING GOALS:

- **To be able to match pronouns and verbs**

- **To recognize collective nouns and be able to match them with verbs**

- **To be able to match verbs and special kinds of words**

In Chapter 2 you learned that nouns may be singular (meaning one) or plural (meaning more than one). To form the plural of most nouns you learned to add s to the end of the word:

Singular	Plural
dog	dogs
cigar	cigars
bottle	bottles

In Chapter 3 you learned that nouns may be replaced by pronouns:

Noun	Pronoun
cigar	it
Mr. Johnson	he
Sarah	she
Bill and I	we
Bill and Harry	they

When you can replace a noun with the pronoun <u>he</u>, <u>she</u>, or <u>it</u>, the

58

verb used with the pronoun in the present tense ends with s. Here are some examples:

The water splatters over everything.
It splatters over everything.

Mrs. Johnson wears pink lipstick.
She wears pink lipstick.

When a noun is plural, you do not add s to the verb. That is, if you can use the pronoun they, you do not add s to the verb:

The construction workers work hard.
They work hard.

The pork chops look burnt.
They look burnt.

Here are two general rules you can follow to match nouns and verbs in the present tense:
1. If the noun ends in s (that is, if it is plural), do not add s to the verb.
2. If the noun does not end in s (that is, if it is singular), add s to the present tense of the verb.

Try It

Read each sentence and decide whether or not the underlined verb or verbs go correctly with the noun or pronoun. If necessary, add s to the underlined verbs.

1. Tom enjoy crackers.
2. He buy crackers by the pound.
3. The cracker break as he butters it.
4. The butter taste better than the cracker does.
5. The cracker crumble as he chew it.
6. The crumbs crunch beneath his feet.
7. An old woman own the hand laundry on the corner.
8. Harrison work in a toothpick factory.
9. The waiter collect more money in tips than he does in pay.
10. He comb his Afro as he talk.

COLLECTIVE NOUNS

Some nouns are tricky. They seem to be plural, but they are really singular. One of these tricky nouns is money. Money is the name for a lot of different things all together—pennies, dollars, quarters, dimes, and nickels. But we also talk about money to mean one thing.

Nouns like money are called COLLECTIVE NOUNS. They are thought of as one thing even though they are made up of many things. Collective nouns can be replaced by the pronoun it. Because of that, a verb ending with s is used with a collective noun to show present action:

> Money disappears too fast.
> It disappears too fast.

Some other collective nouns are family, jury, team, group, committee, and tribe. All these words can be replaced by it, and all take a verb ending in s to show present action.

Try It

In each blank, write the correct present form of the verb in parentheses.

1. The family next door (have) _____ three radios, five children, two dogs, and a canary.

2. My Tuesday night bowling team always (lose) _____ .

3. The Parents Association's committee (meet) _____ every Thursday.

4. The jury (decide) _____ whether a person is innocent.

5. The Indian tribe (work) _____ hard to make the dry land grow crops.

6. The finance committee (take) _____ care of the union dues.

7. The neighborhood group (hope) _____ it can improve garbage collection on the block.

<u>AND</u> WITH SINGULAR NOUNS

The word and often joins together two singular nouns: "the mop and the broom," "hunger and pain."

Look carefully at the verb endings in these sentences. The verbs are underlined.

> José and his girlfriend <u>like</u> potato chips.
> The cat and the dog <u>chase</u> each other.
> Tea and coffee <u>taste</u> great with cinnamon.

None of the verbs in these sentences ends with s. Why? <u>And</u> makes the two singular nouns become a plural noun. Plural nouns can be replaced by the pronoun <u>they</u>. Verbs used with <u>they</u> do not end with <u>s</u>.

> They <u>like</u> potato chips.
> They <u>chase</u> each other.
> They <u>taste</u> great with cinnamon.

Try It

In each blank, write the correct form of the verb in parentheses.

1. Andrea and Pete (like) _____ folk rock music.
2. The mechanic and his girlfriend (do) _____ nothing but drink black coffee and talk.
3. Cola and root beer (cost) _____ the same amount at McGary's.
4. On hot mornings, the husband and wife (get) _____ out of bed early.
5. Slate and his mother (eat) _____ pizza every Friday night.
6. Guards and policemen (be) _____ blocking all the exits.

WORDS LIKE <u>ONE OF</u>

There is a group of words that often come before plural nouns in a sentence. They tell <u>how many</u>. These words often end with <u>of</u>: one of, each one of, any of, any one of, every, either one of, neither one of.

All these words mean a single thing. They are like singular nouns. Look carefully at how these words are used in sentences.

> <u>One of</u> the detectives looks for fingerprints.
> <u>Each one of</u> the holes was plugged with newspaper.
> <u>Every</u> man here wants a cup of coffee.
> <u>Neither one of</u> the stores is open.

The verb following groups of words like <u>one of</u> ends with <u>s</u>. This is because the words <u>one of the detectives</u> can be replaced by the pronoun <u>he</u>. Verbs that follow <u>he</u> end with <u>s</u>.

Try It

Fill each blank with the correct form of the verb in parentheses. Make all the verbs present tense.

1. Every man (speak) _____ well of him.
2. Any friend of yours (be) _____ a friend of mine.

3. Every person in the room (be) _____ talking at once.

4. Neither one of the men (run) _____ the shop.

5. Every child on the block (shine) _____ shoes.

6. I'm sure any drugstore (sell) _____ it.

7. One of the bottles (be) _____ cracked.

8. Each one of the clerks (have) _____ trouble making change.

9. Every supermarket in the city (carry) _____ low-phosphate detergents.

10. Only one of the old gang (be) _____ single.

WORDS WITH -BODY OR -ONE

There is another group of words that are used to mean one person. These words end with -body or -one. Here are the ones that are used most often:

anybody	anyone
everybody	everyone
nobody	no one
somebody	someone

Since these words mean only one person, the verbs that follow them end with s.

Anybody who wants my car can have it.
Everyone loves him.
Nobody cares.
Somebody loves me.

Try It

Fill each blank with the correct form of the verb in parentheses. Make all the verbs present tense.

1. Anyone who (have) _____ the cash can play.

2. Everybody (want) _____ one.

3. Nobody (talk) _____ as much as he does.

4. Someone always (put) _____ sugar in my coffee.

5. Everyone (do) _____ as he pleases.

6. Anybody who (say) _____ that is a liar.

7. No one (know) _____ why he did it.

8. Nobody (go) _____ there any more.

9. Somebody (be) _____ trying to help him.

10. Yes, everybody (be) _____ invited.

NEITHER AND EITHER

You have seen how to use neither one of and either one of. Neither and either are special words, and they are used in another way, too. When neither or either is used in a sentence, another small word goes with it. Nor goes with neither, and or goes with either.

> Neither the smell nor the color appeals to me.
> Either red or blue is fine.

There are three things you must understand to use neither and either correctly.

1. If both nouns in the first part of the sentence are singular, use a verb that ends with s:

> Either the cat or the dog is under the bed.

As you can see, both the nouns in the sentence are singular: cat and dog. The verb that follows them and shows present action ends with s: is.

2. If both nouns in the first part of the sentence are plural, use a verb that does not end with s:

> Neither the men nor the women like the party.

Men and women are both plural, and the verb does not end with s.

3. If there is one singular and one plural noun, the verb form depends on the noun closest to the verb:

> Neither the students nor the teacher knows the answer.
> Neither the teacher nor the students know the answer.

In each sentence, there is one singular and one plural noun. In the first sentence, teacher is the noun closest to the verb. Teacher is singular, so the correct verb form ends with s. In the second sentence, students is the noun closest to the verb. Students is plural, so the correct verb form does not end with s.

Try It

Fill each blank with the correct form of the verb in parentheses. The action of each sentence is in the present.

1. Don't argue. Either you or he (lose) _____.

2. Neither the sink nor the tub (work) _____.

3. Neither Republicans nor Democrats (see) _____ it my way.

4. I don't, but I think Lurleen or John (do) _____.

5. It's either the drains or the heating that (break) _____ down regularly.

6. Either Main Street or Broadway (take) _____ you to the freeway.

7. Neither the truck driver nor the bus driver (say) _____ he is to blame for the accident.

8. Neither the hot tea nor the blankets (make) _____ him feel any warmer.

9. Either the police or the National Guard (be) _____ to be sent back.

10. It's either your picture tube or your tuning knobs that (need) _____ repair.

WORDS LIKE <u>ALL</u>

Another group of words that sometimes gives people trouble is a group of little words that mean more than one. Some of them are underlined in the sentences below.

> <u>All</u> the men laugh at his funny stories.
> <u>Several</u> members give five dollars every year.
> <u>Many</u> women have their hair done every Saturday.

Each of these words is followed by a verb that does not end with <u>s</u>.

> All ... laugh ...
> Several ... give ...
> Many ... have ...

Try It

Fill each blank with the correct form of the verb in parentheses. Each verb should show present action. As you do this exercise, remember the other words you have studied in this chapter.

1. Several people in the audience always (clap) _____ at the wrong time.

2. Anybody who (do) _____, doesn't understand music.

3. All the players (look) _____ annoyed when it happens.

4. Somebody (say) _____, "Sssh."

5. Many of the ushers (sit) _____ in the empty seats during the performance.

6. One of the people behind me always (seem) _____ to be whispering.

7. It seems as if everybody (sneeze) _____ at least once during the performance.

8. A few of the smokers (move) _____ to the balcony to smoke.

9. Every empty seat in the front row (be) _____ soon filled.

10. Each player (smile) _____ as he or she bows.

HERE AND THERE

Here and there tell where.

> Here is your money.
> There are your tools.

A form of the verb be usually goes with here and there. The forms of be are is, are, am, was, and were. The noun that goes with these forms of be can be singular or plural, like money or tools.

If the noun is singular, the verb must be is or was.

> There is your belt.
> Your belt was there yesterday.

If the noun is plural, the verb must be are or were.

> Here are your shoes.
> Your shoes were here yesterday.

If the pronoun I is in the sentence, the verb must be am if it is happening now, or was if it has already happened.

> Here I am.
> I was there yesterday.

Try It

Before each sentence, the word in parentheses tells you when the action in the sentence happens. Put the correct form of <u>be</u> in each blank.

(present)   1. Here ＿＿＿＿＿ the receipts.

(present)   2. There ＿＿＿＿＿ no second chances.

(present)   3. Here it ＿＿＿＿＿.

(past)   4. His tie ＿＿＿＿＿ over there the last time I saw it.

(past)   5. There ＿＿＿＿＿ my pocketbook, right where I had left it.

(past)   6. There I ＿＿＿＿＿ without my umbrella.

Try It in a Paragraph

Read the story below. Decide whether or not each underlined verb matches the noun or pronoun it follows. If it doesn't match, choose the correct verb from the choices lettered (a) to (d) on the right-hand side of the page. Blacken the space next to your letter choice. Choice (a) is always the same as the underlined verb in the story. The action in the story takes place in the present.

               1

Several men <u>are standing</u> outside a store.

1. (a)| | are standing

   (b)| | have stood

   (c)| | is standing

   (d)| | stood

               2

One of the men <u>say</u> that he can take anything from the store without being seen.

2. (a)| | say

   (b)| | will say

   (c)| | says

   (d)| | saying

               3   4

All the men in the group <u>laughing</u> and <u>said</u> he can't.

3. (a)| | laughing

   (b)| | laughs

   (c)| | laugh

   (d)| | laughed

4. (a)| | said

(b)| | saids

(c)| | say

(d)| | says

5
Somebody even <u>are betting</u> him $20 that he can't take

a box of cigars from the store.

5. (a)| | are betting

(b)| | bet

(c)| | bets

(d)| | betted

6
The man <u>agrees</u> to the bet and goes into the store with

7
the man who <u>has</u> the $20.

6. (a)| | agrees

(b)| | agree

(c)| | agreed

(d)| | are agree

7. (a)| | has

(b)| | have

(c)| | had

(d)| | haves

8
All the other men <u>wait</u> outside.

8. (a)| | wait

(b)| | waiting

(c)| | waits

(d)| | waited

9
The men <u>looks</u> around the store.

9. (a)| | looks

(b)| | looked

(c)| | is looking

(d)| | look

A box of cigars <u>are</u>¹⁰ on a shelf in the back of the store.

10. (a)| |are

(b)| |is

(c)| |be

(d)| |will be

The first man <u>is taking</u>¹¹ the box and walks out.

11. (a)| |is taking

(b)| |take

(c)| |takes

(d)| |took

"Here it <u>are</u>¹²!" he says proudly.

12. (a)| |are

(b)| |am

(c)| |was

(d)| |is

"I <u>win</u>¹³ the bet!"

13. (a)| |win

(b)| |had won

(c)| |has won

(d)| |winning

The man with the $20 smiles. "You <u>is</u>¹⁴ very smart," he answers.

14. (a)| |is

(b)| |are

(c)| |am

(d)| |were

"But I <u>is</u>¹⁵ a detective, and you are under arrest for shoplifting."

15. (a)| |is

(b)| |are

(c)| |am

(d)| |was

10. MORE ABOUT PRONOUNS

Pronouns change when they are used in different parts of a sentence. Look at this sentence. Then circle the pronoun in the sentence.

Maggie loves me.

Me is the pronoun.

Circle the pronouns in the following sentences.

1. Maggie loves me.
2. Maggie loves them.
3. Maggie loves us.
4. Maggie loves it.
5. Maggie loves her.
6. Maggie loves you.

The pronouns are (1) me, (2) them, (3) us, (4) it, (5) her, (6) you.

These pronouns come after certain verbs that seem unfinished without a noun or pronoun following them. If you read "Maggie loves," you would ask, "Maggie loves whom?" or, "Maggie loves what?" There are many verbs that are like love. Some of them are underlined in these sentences:

He threw it.
She slapped him.
They really gave it to us.
You bought her a rose.
We saw you.

These "unfinished" verbs do something to, with, or for a thing or a person. The only pronouns that can follow these verbs are:

me	you
you	us
him, her, it	them

Try It

Choose the correct pronoun to replace the word or words in parentheses before each blank. Write the pronoun in the blank.

1. (Her boy friend) _____ promised her the moon, but he gave (the woman) _____ a bottle of perfume instead.

2. We heard that (Jack and Sue) _____ went on vacation to see whether (Jack and Sue) _____ could still relax.

3. He gave (Fred and I) _____ a barrel of water and a diving board so (Fred and I) _____ could practice our act.

4. (Ernie) _____ knew that they would be waiting for (Ernie) _____ .

5. I closed (the letter) _____ with tape.

6. He told (Juan and I) _____ not to swim in the river because (the river) _____ looked too dirty.

7. (Carol) _____ made us feel the grass because (Carol) _____ said (the grass) _____ felt like velvet.

8. You took (I) _____ on a midnight walk through the mud so (you and I) _____ could hear the frogs croak in the darkness?

9. The grower paid (my friends and I) _____ less than he promised us (the grower) _____ would.

USING BE WITH I

> "Is this a picture of you?"
> "Yes. That is me."
> "That's bad grammar."
> "I know it. But it's a bad picture."

In written English "That is me" is incorrect. Of course, everyone says "That's me" when he speaks. In fact, it sounds funny to say "That's I" or "It's I." But, nevertheless, "It is I" is correct.

As you learned before, the verb be in all its forms is special. Unlike the other verbs, be is followed by the pronouns I, he, she, it, you, we, and they.

> It was he.
> It is she.
> It had been they.
> It will be you.

Try It

Choose the pronoun that replaces the word in parentheses before each blank. Put the correct pronoun in the blank.

1. I don't think it was (the man) _____ who shoved me.
2. If it were (the people) _____, they certainly wouldn't like it.
3. She wondered what she would have done if it had been (the woman) _____.
4. If it were (I) _____, I wouldn't stand for it.
5. It was (my wife and I) _____ who called the police.
6. It was (the girl) _____ who stayed up all night.

USING "REVERSIBLE" PRONOUNS

Some pronouns turn the action of the verb back on the thing talked about in the sentence. They reverse the action:

> I burned myself.
> He blamed himself.
> The children hurt themselves.

The "reversible" pronoun must show that it is the same as the thing talked about. You would not say "I fooled himself." But you could say any of these:

> I fooled myself.
> You fooled yourself.
> She fooled herself.
> He fooled himself.
> It fooled itself.
> We fooled ourselves.
> They fooled themselves.
> You fooled yourselves. [Yourselves means
>   more than one person.]

Look at these pronouns carefully and learn them. Don't make the mistake of saying hisself or theirselves.

Try It

Put the correct "reversible" pronoun in each blank.

1. "I can look after _____," she said.
2. "Don't get angry, Jesse. Be cool," Jesse said to _____.
3. "I'll have a glass _____," he said.

4. They started taking in laundry to support _____.

5. Although we need some money, we won't ask for it _____.

6. They locked _____ out.

7. If it rains all day, you and your kids won't know what to do with _____.

8. "Get it _____," she snapped. "Can't you see I'm busy?"

9. We wrapped _____ in the warmest blankets we could find, while the radiator hissed and gurgled to _____.

10. The bellhop whistled to _____ as he carried her baggage onto the elevator.

WHO'S "HE"?

Read this sentence:

> Hector told Eugene that he had parked the car in a no-parking zone.

Who parked the car? The pronoun he doesn't tell you. In this sentence, either Hector or Eugene could have parked it. You would know who he was if the sentence were changed to this:

> Hector told Eugene that Eugene had parked the car in a no-parking zone.

A pronoun should show clearly which noun it replaces. The noun should be in the same sentence with the pronoun, or in a sentence right before or after the pronoun.

> The neon signs at night hurt Hector's eyes, so he wore sunglasses.

In that sentence the pronoun comes after the noun in the same sentence. He replaces Hector.

In the first sentence below, the pronoun (they) is in the same sentence with the noun it replaces (men). In the second sentence, the pronoun them also replaces men. That pronoun is in the sentence right after the sentence with the noun.

> When we found the lost men, they were exhausted.
> We had not heard them call for several hours.

Try It in a Paragraph

Read the story below. Decide whether or not the underlined pronouns are used correctly. If they are not correct, choose the correct pronouns from the choices lettered (a) to (d) on the right-hand side of the page. Blacken the space next to your letter choice. Choice (a) is always the same as the underlined pronouns in the story.

Jesse and Slate went to visit a husband and wife who lived in New York City. While there, Jesse told this story to <u>they</u>:
     ¹

1. (a)| | they
   (b)| | their
   (c)| | them
   (d)| | they're

We wanted to buy some fruit for <u>you and she</u>, so we went into a fancy fruit shop.
     ²

2. (a)| | you and she
   (b)| | you and her
   (c)| | yous
   (d)| | you's

The owner tried to sell some grapes to Slate and <u>I</u>, but I wanted some apples. The grapes cost $1.50 a pound!
     ³

3. (a)| | I
   (b)| | us
   (c)| | me
   (d)| | we

"Oh," the owner said. "I don't want to sell the apples to <u>you and him</u>. They're not so good."
     ⁴

4. (a)| | you and him
   (b)| | you and he
   (c)| | yous
   (d)| | them

The grapes didn't look good to either Slate or <u>us</u>, so we bought a half dozen pears.
     ⁵

5. (a)| | us
   (b)| | I
   (c)| | you
   (d)| | me

"That will be $1.75, sir," the owner said to <u>us</u>.⁶

6. (a)| | us

   (b)| | you

   (c)| | them

   (d)| | we

"For a half dozen pears?" I asked.

"Yes," he said.

Angry, I gave the money to <u>he</u>⁷, took the pears with <u>him</u>⁸, and started to walk out.

7. (a)| |he

   (b)| |you

   (c)| |his

   (d)| |him

8. (a)| |him

   (b)| |you

   (c)| |we

   (d)| |us

"Wait. You forgot your change, sir," the owner called after <u>we</u>⁹.

"Never mind. You keep it," I called back. "I stepped on a grape on the way in."

9. (a)| |we

   (b)| |us

   (c)| |he

   (d)| |them

11. DESCRIBING AND COMPARING (ADJECTIVES)

National Coal Association

Some words describe nouns and pronouns. These words are called ADJECTIVES. They tell what kind, how much, or how many.

LEARNING GOALS:

- **To identify adjectives**

- **To use who, which, and that correctly**

- **To compare two or more kinds of things**

One <u>young</u> man looks up at the <u>huge</u> crane.

In the sentence above, the word <u>one</u> tells how many men there are; <u>young</u> describes what kind of man he is; and <u>huge</u> tells what kind of crane it is or how it looks.

Adjectives help make what we say more interesting and accurate. Look at these pairs of sentences:

I have a car.
I have a <u>new</u>, <u>sporty</u> car.

The man told a story.
The <u>old</u> man told a <u>frightening</u> story.

In each case, the second sentence is more interesting and accurate than the first.

Try It

Underline the adjectives in the following sentences.

1. Six policemen stopped a small car.
2. When the first snow fell, we were still wearing our light coats.
3. We made a bad mistake when we bought a white rug.
4. If you buy fresh vegetables, wash them carefully in cold water.
5. This is a short movie.

WHO, WHICH, THAT

Sometimes more than one word is used to describe a noun. The words who, which, and that help other words point out or identify people or things. They work like adjectives because they describe nouns and often tell what kind. Look at the way who, which, and that are used in the following sentences:

> The women, who were brave, whistled back at the construction workers.
>
> The dog, which is our neighbor's, is a terrier.
>
> An old lady kept a parrot that was always swearing.

The word who is used only to point out people.
The word which is used only to point out animals and things.
The word that is used to point out animals, things, and sometimes people.

Try It

Put who, which, or that in each blank in the following sentences.

1. I hate people _____ are grouchy.
2. My car, _____ was bought new, needs repair work.
3. There was once a woman _____ worked at a job for fifty-two years and never missed a day.
4. The famous man, _____ wrote a book about marriage, got divorced.
5. I like men _____ wear alligator shoes.
6. The crow _____ was chewing up parking tickets was sentenced to thirty days.
7. The dog on Fifth Avenue _____ was tied to a parking meter barked at everyone _____ walked by.

8. The landlady _____ hated dogs did not let animals
_____ were not housebroken into her apartment building.

9. The store owner, _____ had been warned by the Health
Department, made a sign _____ said "No Animals Allowed."

10. There is the cat _____ caught the rat.

-ER AND -EST

Adjectives often describe nouns and pronouns by comparing them with something else. These adjectives tell how much greater, better, smaller, or prettier one thing is than another. Look at this sentence:

> The eight tall men drank colder soda than the seven
> short women drank.

The word colder compares two kinds of soda, the men's soda and the women's soda. It tells you that the men's soda was not as warm as the women's.

Look at this sentence. If the waiters also were drinking cold soda, we could say:

> The six waiters drank the coldest soda of all.

That sentence tells that the waiters' soda was the coldest of all three kinds of soda.

Adjectives that end with -er compare two things. Adjectives that end with -est compare three or more things.

> Your motorcycle is faster than mine.
> But his motorcycle is the fastest of all three.

Look again at the second sentence above and notice that the word the is used before the word that ends with -est.

MORE AND MOST

Some adjectives that describe nouns and pronouns don't end with -er or -est when they compare things. Instead, these words use more or the most. For example:

> This chair is more comfortable than that one.
> But the sofa is the most comfortable seat in the room.

The word more, like the ending -er, is used to compare two things. The most, like the ending -est, is used to compare three or more things.

You are probably wondering when you use more or the most before a word and when you add -er or -est to the end of a word. Generally, when the adjective is a short one, it ends with -er or -est. Longer words have more or the most before them.

Here are examples of short adjectives that end with -er or -est:

Describing one thing	Comparing two things	Comparing three or more things
fresh	fresher	the freshest
slow	slower	the slowest
short	shorter	the shortest
big	bigger	the biggest
old	older	the oldest
long	longer	the longest
small	smaller	the smallest

Here are examples of longer adjectives that have more or the most before them:

Describing one thing	Comparing two things	Comparing three or more things
difficult	more difficult	the most difficult
dangerous	more dangerous	the most dangerous
likable	more likable	the most likable
careless	more careless	the most careless
valuable	more valuable	the most valuable
beautiful	more beautiful	the most beautiful

Do not use both -er and more or -est and most together in comparing. Do not write more fresher or most slowest.

Try It

Fill each blank with the correct form of the word in parentheses. (The words in parentheses are different ways to say "funny.")

1. Eddie is a (funny) _____ man.
2. Mac is (amusing) _____ than Eddie.
3. Larry is (witty) _____ man I know.
4. Ina is so (jolly) _____ she makes everyone happy.
5. Bea is (jovial) _____ than Ina.

SPECIAL WORDS

There are other adjectives that describe nouns and pronouns and tell how much. These words compare two or more things, but they do not end in -er or -est, and they do not use more or the most before them. These words change their spelling to show how much.

Describing one thing	Comparing two things	Comparing three or more things
good	better	the best
bad	worse	the worst
far	farther	the farthest
little	less	the least

Try It

Fill each blank with the correct form of the word in parentheses.

1. He has traveled (far) _____ of all the visitors.

2. This "improved" instant coffee is (bad) _____ than the old one.

3. This is (good) _____ movie I've seen in a long time.

4. You gave me (little) _____ money than you gave him.

5. It's just too (bad) _____ to talk about.

USING THAN TO COMPARE THINGS

Another way of comparing two things is by using the word than.

> I like her better than he does.
> She likes him better than me.

A pronoun follows the word than in each sentence above. In the first sentence, the pronoun after than is he. In the second sentence, the pronoun after than is me.

When the word than is used, one or two words often have been left out of the sentence.

> She likes him better than me.
> She likes him better than (she likes) me.

The words that were left out are she likes. Whom does she like less? She likes me less.

Here is another example:

> I am more careful than he.
> I am more careful than he (is).

The word that is missing is is. Who is less careful? He is.

Sometimes the verb does or do follows the pronoun that comes after than. Always use the pronouns I, you, we, he, she, it, and they before does or do.

> Hector eats more than he does.
> They both eat more than we do.

Try It

Decide what pronoun should replace the noun in parentheses before each blank. Put the correct pronoun in the blank in each sentence.

1. She frowns more than (her husband) _____ does.

2. He scowls at the boss more than at (the workers) _____.

3. I smile more often than (my friends) _____ do.

4. I have noticed that my little boy grins less than (my little girl) _____ does.

5. The puppies cry louder than (the babies) _____.

Try It in a Paragraph

Read each story below. Decide whether or not the underlined words are used correctly. If they are not, choose the correct words from the choices lettered (a) to (c) or (a) to (d) on the right-hand side of the page. Blacken the space next to your letter choice. Choice (a) is always the same as the underlined words in the story.

STORY 1:

The owner of a toy store had Santa Claus "visit" each year so that parents could bring their children to see him. One evening just before Christmas, the owner, which¹ wanted everything to be perfect, saw a young boy that² seemed to be about seven years old dragging a big sack down an aisle.

1. (a) | | which
   (b) | | that
   (c) | | who

2. (a) | | that
   (b) | | who
   (c) | | which

Another little boy was following behind, pushing the
sack <u>which</u> his friend was pulling.
³

3. (a)| | which

   (b)| | what

   (c)| | who

"What are you boys doing here getting in the way of
all these people <u>which</u> want to buy presents?" asked
⁴
the angry owner. "If you don't stop getting in the way,
Santa Claus will not bring you anything for Christmas."

The boy pulling the bag, <u>who</u> was shaking violently,
⁵
said as he walked past the owner, "<u>Who</u> do you think
⁶
is in this bag?"

4. (a)| | which

   (b)| | what

   (c)| | who

5. (a)| | who

   (b)| | what

   (c)| | which

6. (a)| | Who

   (b)| | Which

   (c)| | That

STORY 2:

Three friends were driving to a ball game in a <u>newer</u>
¹
car. Two of the men sat in the front seat, and <u>the most</u>
²
<u>oldest</u> man sat in the back.

1. (a)| | newer

   (b)| | more newer

   (c)| | new

   (d)| | the newest

2. (a)| | the most oldest

   (b)| | the more oldest

   (c)| | the oldest

   (d)| | the more older

The driver was a <u>more good</u> driver,[3] and he liked to drive fast. The car raced along the road. Soon the car came to a railroad crossing. The three men saw a train coming around the bend.

Right then the two men in the front seat began to argue. The <u>more foolish</u>[4] of the two said the car could beat the train. He was the driver. The other man, who was <u>more wiser than</u>[5] the driver, said the car couldn't.

"Don't get excited," said the driver. "This car is <u>the better</u>[6][7] car on the road. I tell you I can easily do <u>more good</u> than that train."

"And I tell you, you can't," shouted the other. "A train is <u>the fastest</u>[8] thing on wheels. It can go faster <u>than us</u>.[9]

3. (a) | | more good

   (b) | | good

   (c) | | gooder

   (d) | | best

4. (a) | | more foolish

   (b) | | foolisher

   (c) | | most foolish

   (d) | | foolish

5. (a) | | more wiser than

   (b) | | wisest than

   (c) | | wiser than

   (d) | | the more wiser than

6. (a) | | the better

   (b) | | the more better

   (c) | | the gooder

   (d) | | the best

7. (a) | | more good

   (b) | | the better

   (c) | | better

   (d) | | gooder

8. (a) | | the fastest

   (b) | | the faster

   (c) | | the most fast

   (d) | | the more faster

9. (a)| | than us.

(b)| | than we.

(c)| | than it.

(d)| | than them.

The argument got <u>loudest</u>, and the speedometer went
¹⁰
<u>higher</u>.
¹¹

10. (a)| | loudest

(b)| | more louder

(c)| | louder

(d)| | the most loud

11. (a)| | higher.

(b)| | high.

(c)| | the highest.

(d)| | more higher.

Finally the man in the back seat, who was quieter <u>than</u>
¹²
<u>them</u>, could stand it no longer.

"Well," he said. "I don't care who wins this race, but
I hope it isn't a tie!"

12. (a)| | than them

(b)| | than us

(c)| | than they

(d)| | than he

12. HOOKING WORDS (PREPOSITIONS)

LEARNING GOALS:

• To identify prepositions

• To know what pronouns to use after prepositions

Some small words "hook" other words together. Look at the underlined words below:

> barrels of pickles
> locked in the closet
> standing on the corner
> came from the cracks in the wall
> works at the factory
> found by the door
> flew to the moon
> something for you
> said with tears

The nine small words of, in, on, from, at, by, to, for, and with are hooking words called PREPOSITIONS. They hook ideas or actions to one another.

The hooking word and the words that follow it tell more about the verb or noun that comes before them.

> I shipped ten barrels.
> I shipped ten barrels of salt.

The words of salt tell more about the barrels. They tell what was in the barrels.

> He ran.
> He ran down the street.

The hooking word in the second sentence is down. The words down the street tell more about the verb ran. They tell where he ran.

Try It

Underline the hooking words in the following sentence.

> • With the addition of *vitamin D* to milk, rickets has been virtually eliminated.

Hooking words connect groups of words in several ways:

1. They show <u>where</u>:

at my side	around the country	above the fireplace
by my heart	within the jail cell	across the street
in my hand	into the house	against the wall
on my foot	onto the bicycle	beside her husband
among the leaves	inside the prison	outside the station

2. They show <u>direction</u>:

to the store	off my back
from heaven	through the tunnel
up the stairs	out the door
down the slide	toward the lake

3. They show <u>relationships</u> among people:

of ours	between you and me
for you	with us

4. They show <u>when</u>:

by dawn	during the night
after lunch	at midnight
until dusk	before noon

As you can see, some prepositions can be used in more than one way. Incorrect use of a preposition can come about for two reasons:
1. The pronoun or pronouns that follow a hooking word are not correct.
2. The verb that follows the noun after the hooking word <u>of</u> does not have the right ending.

Here is an example and explanation of the first kind of mistake. This sentence is incorrect:

He bought plastic combs for she and I.

This sentence is correct:

He bought plastic combs for her and me.

The pronouns that come after prepositions are always <u>me</u>, <u>him</u>, <u>her</u>, <u>it</u>, <u>you</u>, <u>us</u>, <u>them</u>, and <u>whom</u>. <u>For</u> is the preposition in the sentence above. The pronouns that come after <u>for</u> are <u>her</u> and <u>me</u>. (To learn more about these pronouns, turn to page 69.)

Try It

Fill each blank with the correct pronoun based on the word in parentheses before each blank.

1. Listen, between you and (I) _____, she's lying.
2. Don't give it to her or (Don) _____.
3. Do you want to come with (my husband and I) _____?
4. She won't do it for either (she) _____ or me.
5. You say you're their friend, and yet you gossip about (the husband and his wife) _____.

Here is an example and explanation of the second kind of mistake. This sentence is incorrect:

A barrel of pickles roll down the hill.

This sentence is correct:

A barrel of pickles rolls down the hill.

The hooking word is <u>of</u>. The words <u>of pickles</u> describe what is in the barrel. They are not the thing talked about in the sentence. The verb must go with the noun that comes before <u>of</u>. In this sentence, the noun is <u>barrel</u>. <u>Barrel</u> can be replaced by the pronoun <u>it</u>. <u>It</u> is always followed by a verb that ends with <u>s</u>, so the verb in this sentence is <u>rolls</u>.

Try It Again

Fill each blank with the correct form of the verb in parentheses.

1. The piece of pizza (be) _____ warm a few minutes ago.
2. Here (be) _____ a carton of soda.
3. There (be) _____ six cans of root beer in the refrigerator.
4. Eight boxes of lunch (come) _____ every day at noon.
5. Yes, all of us (do) _____.
6. Two spots of color (burn) _____ in her cheeks.

Try It in a Paragraph

Read the story on page 87. Decide whether or not the underlined words are used correctly. If they are not, choose the correct word from the choices on the right-hand side of the page. Blacken the space next to your letter choice. Choice (a) is always the same as the underlined word in the story. This story is in the present tense.

A man of about forty $\overset{1}{\underline{were}}$ telling his problems to a friend.

1. (a)| | were

   (b)| | was

   (c)| | is

   (d)| | are

"One of my problems $\overset{2}{\underline{are}}$ my 250-acre estate with a golf course, swimming pool, tennis court, and eight-car garage.

2. (a)| | are

   (b)| | is

   (c)| | was

   (d)| | were

"Another one of the things that $\overset{3}{\underline{is}}$ driving me crazy $\overset{4}{\underline{are}}$ my airplane, yacht, and stable of horses.

3. (a)| | is

   (b)| | are

   (c)| | was

   (d)| | were

4. (a)| | are

   (b)| | is

   (c)| | was

   (d)| | were

"One of my sons $\overset{5}{\underline{are}}$ in college and my daughters $\overset{6}{\underline{is}}$ attending a private school in England."

5. (a)| | are

   (b)| | is

   (c)| | was

   (d)| | were

The friend interrupts the man by saying, "Why are you complaining? It seems to me you have a perfect setup."

6. (a)| | is

   (b)| | are

   (c)| | was

   (d)| | were

"It is wonderful," said the man, "except that I, of all people, only <u>makes</u> $47.35 a week."

7

7. (a)| | makes

(b)| | made

(c)| | have made

(d)| | make

13. WORDS THAT DESCRIBE VERBS (ADVERBS)

Some words describe verbs. They are called ADVERBS, and they tell how, where, or when.

LEARNING
GOALS:

- **To identify adverbs**

- **To learn how to form adverbs**

Read the story below and look carefully at the underlined words.

> A man got a job running an elevator. The first time he ran it, it went up all right, but when it came down it stopped too suddenly.
>
> "Man," he said, turning to the passengers, "did I stop too quickly?"
>
> "No, no," said a six-footer, "you didn't stop too quickly. I always wear my necktie around my hips."

WORDS THAT TELL HOW

The words suddenly and quickly are adverbs that describe how or in what way an action happens. These adverbs often end in -ly:

> The tramp snored quietly.
> Maria answered softly.
> José worked carefully.

Other words or groups of words that tell how or in what way do not end in -ly:

> He ran fast.
> He tried hard.
> He walked straight.
> She sang well.
> I shut the door with a bang.

WORDS THAT TELL WHERE

Look at these sentences:

> I live here.
> Don't go there.
> The pigeon is underneath the chair.

The underlined words tell where. <u>Here</u> tells where I live. <u>There</u> tells where you should not go. <u>Underneath the chair</u> tells where the pigeon is. You can see that adverbs may be made up of groups of words beginning with prepositions.

WORDS THAT TELL <u>WHEN</u>

Some adverbs tell when or during what time the action took place.

He bought a used coat <u>yesterday</u>.

The word <u>yesterday</u> answers the question, "When did he buy the coat?"

Try It

Put -<u>ly</u> on the word in each sentence that tells <u>how</u> the action happened.
1. Sudden I felt old and used up.
2. She undid the chain and opened the door slow.
3. He just sat there, silent looking down when I looked up and looking up when I looked down.
4. The hobo walked up to a man and said polite, "Will you give me a dime for a cup of coffee?"
5. The man walked away quick.
6. He drove so rapid that he got into an accident.
7. He sneezed loud.

Try It

Underline the adverb or adverbs in each sentence. Remember that an adverb tells how, where, or when.
1. The man had to run fast and hard to win the race.
2. The men left in a hurry when the police came.
3. The woman smiled warmly.
4. Your shoes are not there.
5. He wisely turned down the offer.

Try It Again

Underline the adverbs in the following item.

Additives for health: In the 1920's, *iodine* was added to salt to eliminate the iodine deficiency in the goiter belt in the Great Lakes area. Incidence of goiter dropped dramatically....

Try It in a Paragraph

Read the story below. Decide whether or not each underlined word is used correctly. If it is not correct, choose the correct word from the choices lettered (a) to (d) on the right. Blacken the space next to your choice. Choice (a) is always the same as the word in the story.

1. A hobo was walking <u>slow</u> down the street trying to get money for a cup of coffee.

   1. (a) | | slow
      (b) | | slowly
      (c) | | slower
      (d) | | more slow

2. He saw a man coming <u>quickly</u> toward him.

   2. (a) | | quickly
      (b) | | quicker
      (c) | | the quickest
      (d) | | quick

3. "Could you spare fifty cents for a cup of coffee?" the hobo asked <u>more quietly</u>.

   3. (a) | | more quietly
      (b) | | quiet
      (c) | | quieter
      (d) | | quietly

4. "But coffee is only thirty cents a cup," the man said, looking at the hobo <u>suspiciously</u>.

   4. (a) | | suspiciously
      (b) | | suspicious
      (c) | | suspicious like
      (d) | | more suspiciously

5. "I know," the hobo said <u>polite like</u>, "but I always leave a big tip."

   5. (a) | | polite like
      (b) | | politely
      (c) | | polite
      (d) | | more polite

CHECKUP TEST 2

Matching Nouns and Verbs

1. Write <u>T</u> in the blank if the statement is true. Write <u>F</u> if it is false.

    a. _____ Nouns may be singular or plural.

    b. _____ Nouns may be replaced by verbs.

    c. _____ When a noun ends in s, do not add s to the verb.

    d. _____ When a noun does not end in s, do add s to the verb.

    e. _____ <u>The chops looks burnt</u> is a correct sentence.

2. Underline the form of <u>be</u> that fits into the sentence.

    a. Tuesday (was, were) an important day.

    b. The club (was, were) having an election.

    c. Edna, Harry, Victor, and Jane (was, were) the previous officers.

    d. One of the members (was, were) calling for reforms.

    e. She said that neither Edna nor Harry (was, were) a good officer.

3. From the list on the left, choose the form of <u>be</u> that fits into each sentence. Write your choice in the blank in each sentence.

    am   a. Here I _____.

    is   b. There _____ two tables in this room now.

    was   c. There _____ only one chair.

    were   d. I looked for you, and there you _____.

    are   e. _____ Ned in the play last night?

4. Read the paragraph below. From the verbs in parentheses, choose the one that matches the noun or pronoun it follows. Underline your choices.

    a. Many people (is, are, was, will be) unaware that

    b. nutritious, safe, good natural foods (contains, contain, containing, is containing) small amounts of natural toxins. One of the chemicals in potatoes, solanine,

    c. (is, be, wasn't, are) toxic in large amounts.

    d. Cyanide, the poison found in apricot pits, (were, be, is, are)

    e. also found in lima beans; there (is, are, were, be) nitrates in spinach, beets, lettuce, eggplant, celery and turnip greens, as well as in cured meats.

More about Pronouns

5. From the list on the left, pick the pronoun that can replace the word or words in parentheses in each sentence. Write the pronoun in the blank.

she   a. Greta took (a book) _____ from the shelf.

me   b. (Greta) _____ put the book away.

it   c. Give it to (the other women) _____, Greta.

her   d. "No, it's for (Greta) _____," she said.

them   e. But it was not really for (Greta) _____.

6. In each sentence, write a pronoun in the blank that can replace the word in parentheses.

   a. It is (the woman) _____ .
   b. Neither Felix nor (his brother) _____ is going.
   c. "That is (the man) _____ !" shouted the witness.
   d. It was (those people) _____ who were at the party.
   e. It will be (myself) _____ behind that desk someday.

7. Underline the word in parentheses that should be used in each sentence.

   a. He said he could do it (himself, he).
   b. We are old enough to go (us, ourselves).
   c. The hostess, said, "Help (herself, yourselves)."
   d. The cat washed (itself, hisself).
   e. Today I am all by (yourself, myself).

8. Rewrite the following sentences to make their meanings clear. Use two sentences where necessary. (There may be more than one correct way to rewrite some of the sentences. Just choose one.)

   a. The women played cards with the men, and they lost.

   _____

   _____

   b. Maxie asked Homer if he had received a letter.

   _____

   _____

   c. Joanna told her she had to leave.

   _____

   _____

   d. The police chased the crooks. They ran.

   _____

   _____

Describing and Comparing (Adjectives)

9. Underline the adjectives in the picnic menu below.

   a. cold chicken
   b. ripe tomatoes
   c. hardboiled eggs
   d. crunchy apples
   e. hot coffee

10. Write who, which, or that in the blanks in the following sentences.

   a. Dan likes dogs _____ are gentle.
   b. The foreman likes people _____ work hard.
   c. Robert, _____ is my friend, likes to drive.
   d. He has a new car _____ can go fast.
   e. It is the car _____ Jerry wanted to buy.

11. Column one lists some adjectives. In column 2, write the form of each adjective that is used to compare two things. In column 3, write the form used to compare three or more things.

Describing one thing	Comparing two things	Comparing two or more things
a. new	a. _____	a. _____
b. hot	b. _____	b. _____
c. usual	c. _____	c. _____
d. narrow	d. _____	d. _____
e. good	e. _____	e. _____
f. bad	f. _____	f. _____
g. small	g. _____	g. _____
h. beautiful	h. _____	h. _____
i. happy	i. _____	i. _____
j. difficult	j. _____	j. _____

Hooking Words (Prepositions)

12. Underline the preposition in each group of words below.

   a. to the shore
   b. oodles of noodles

c. all for me
d. in the window
e. with love
f. on that day
g. music by the Bee Gees
h. from his friend
i. is at home
j. through the mail

13. In each blank write the correct form of the pronoun in parentheses.

a. to (I) _____
b. for (he) _____
c. between you and (I) _____
d. with (they) _____
e. against (it) _____

14. In each sentence, underline the correct word in parentheses.

a. A jar of cookies (is, are) on the shelf.
b. Next to it (is, are) two cans of honey.
c. A barrel of apples (sit, sits) on the floor.
d. A gang of children (is, are) coming in.
e. Soon all the food (is, will be) gone.

Words that Describe Verbs (Adverbs)

15. Underline the adverb in each sentence. In the blank beside the sentence, tell whether the adverb tells <u>how</u>, <u>where</u>, or <u>when</u>.

a. _____ Yesterday I saw Dennis.
b. _____ He was here.
c. _____ He had dinner at my house.
d. _____ He eats slowly.
e. _____ He chews his food thoroughly.
f. _____ I brought dessert to the table.
g. _____ At that time, he was eating his meat.
h. _____ He smiled cheerfully.
i. _____ "Wait," he said quietly.
j. _____ "Good food should be eaten well."

14. POSSESSIVES

Freida Leinwand from Monkmeyer Press Photo Service

LEARNING GOALS:

- To show possession with <u>has</u> or <u>have</u>

- To show possession with <u>'s</u> or <u>s'</u>

- To show possession with pronouns

- To use <u>each</u>, <u>every</u>, and <u>one</u> with <u>his</u> or <u>her</u>

There are two ways to show that someone has or possesses something:

> Donna <u>has</u> two pairs of pliers.
> Donna<u>'s</u> pliers are made of steel.

You can use the verb <u>has</u> or <u>have</u>, or another verb like <u>owns</u> or <u>possesses</u>. Or you can add the mark (<u>'</u>) and <u>s</u> to the person's name. The mark (<u>'</u>) is called an APOSTROPHE.

> Don <u>has</u> some coffee.
> Don<u>'s</u> coffee is cold.

You also can add <u>'s</u> to singular nouns that are not names:

> the landlord's garbage can

Look carefully at the spelling of the underlined words in the following sentence.

> The big <u>boys</u> tied the little <u>boy's</u> shoelaces together.

The word boy is spelled with two different endings in that sentence. The word boys means more than one boy. The word boy's shows that something belongs to a single boy. The shoelaces belong to the little boy. He possesses them.

Now look carefully at the underlined word in this sentence.

The boys tied all the girls' shoelaces together.

The word girls' also shows possession. But girls also shows that there was more than one girl. To show possession with plural nouns you just add the apostrophe (') after the s.

| the land of the Indians | the Indians' land |
| the wishes of the ladies | the ladies' wishes |

We use 's and s' only to show that something belongs to a living thing or person. To show that something belongs to a thing that is not living, such as a table, spoon, or broom, we use the words of the:

the legs of the table
the handle of the spoon
the straws of the broom

Earlier you learned that there are nouns that show more than one (plural) by changing their spelling, not by adding s. Some of these nouns are woman (women), man (men), and child (children). Nouns like these show possession by adding 's for both singular and plural.

the woman's dress
the women's dresses
the child's balloon
the children's balloons
the man's truck
the men's trucks

Try It

Put an apostrophe (') where it is needed in the sentences below.

1. Is that Eugenes tuna-fish sandwich you're eating?
2. The balloon mans balloons burst.
3. Some things are as plain as peoples noses.
4. The old womans snoring drowned out the preachers voice.
5. The roosters crowed.

6. They say undertakers helpers get paid by the hour now, too.
7. The club had a dance floor the size of somebodys kitchen.
8. The legs of that chair look wobbly.
9. Harrisons father was a plumber.
10. She walked into the mens room by mistake.

PRONOUNS THAT SHOW POSSESSION

Pronouns can also show belonging, or possession. Watch how the pronouns he, she, they, we, it, you, and I change in the sentences below to show possession.

He has cold milk.	His milk is cold.
She had hot tea.	Her tea is hot
They have black coffee.	Their coffee is black.
We have red drapes.	Our drapes are red.
It has a red door.	Its door is red.
You have a good dog.	Your dog is good.
I have a grape soda.	My soda is grape.

Try It

In each blank below, put the correct word that shows possession for the pronoun I, you, he, she, it, we, or they.

1. He placed a straw between _____ lips.
2. I stubbed _____ toe.
3. Then she came around the corner, _____ head covered with a tattered shawl.
4. We were excited as we left _____ neighborhood.
5. They looked across the room at each other, and _____ eyes met.
6. It barked when you called _____ name.
7. "You in there, _____ pizza is here," the delivery boy called through the crack in the door.
8. He brought _____ car to a stop at the side of the road.
9. I've served _____ time.

Here is the way to show possession for the pronouns me, you, her, him, us, and them when the pronoun is not followed by a noun.

They gave it to me.	Now it is mine.
I gave it to you.	Now it is yours.

I gave it to <u>her</u>.   Now it is <u>hers</u>.
I gave it to <u>him</u>.   Now it is <u>his</u>.
They gave it to <u>us</u>.   Now it is <u>ours</u>.
We gave it to <u>them</u>.   Now it is <u>theirs</u>.

See how the spelling changed from the way these pronouns were used before. <u>Their</u> changed to <u>theirs</u>, <u>our</u> to <u>ours</u>, <u>your</u> to <u>yours</u>, <u>her</u> to <u>hers</u>. The letter <u>s</u> was added to the end of each word. The pronoun <u>his</u> stayed the same. The pronoun <u>my</u> became <u>mine</u>. These pronouns are used to answer a question such as, "Whose car is this?" The answer could be, "It is my car," or "It is mine."

Try It

The following conversation was overheard at a picnic after the food had been spread out. Put the words that show possession in the blank spaces. Use the pronouns in parentheses to guide you.

1. Is that (you) _____?

2. Yes, it's (me) _____.

3. Where is (her) _____?

4. It is next to (us) _____.

5. He took (him) _____ with him.

6. (Them) _____ is better than (us) _____.

7. We'd like (us) _____ filled again, please.

8. Who ate (me) _____?

9. Did you drop (you) _____?

10. They didn't get (them) _____.

<u>WHOSE</u>

The word <u>whose</u> is also a pronoun. It shows possession for the pronoun <u>who</u>.

I don't know <u>whose</u> it is.
The man <u>whose</u> car he took is over there.

Try It

Put the pronoun that shows possession for <u>who</u> in each blank space below.

1. _____ tuna-fish sandwich is this?

2. I'd like to know _____ junk this is.

3. _____ did you say this was?

4. He said he didn't know _____ car banged into his.

5. _____ apartment did you stay at?

USING <u>EACH</u>, <u>EVERY</u>, AND <u>ONE</u> WITH <u>HIS</u>

There are certain pronouns such as <u>anyone</u>, <u>anybody</u>, <u>everyone</u>, and <u>someone</u> that are used to mean one person. To show possession for these words, use the pronoun <u>his</u> or <u>her</u>.

<u>Everyone</u> put on <u>his</u> hat.
<u>Each</u> woman took off <u>her</u> coat.
<u>Anybody</u> who doesn't move <u>his</u> car before
    four o'clock will have it towed away.

The pronoun <u>her</u> is used when it is clear that the sentence is telling something about a girl or a woman. The pronoun <u>his</u> is used in sentences about boys and men and sometimes with nouns or pronouns that don't clearly show whether the person talked about is male or female.

<u>Everyone</u> brought <u>his</u> own sandwich.

Sometimes <u>his or her</u> is used when it is not clear whether the person talked about is male or female.

<u>Everyone</u> brought <u>his or her</u> own sandwich.

Try It

(Fill each blank with the correct pronoun)

1. Everyone paid for _____ own lunch.

2. Somebody left _____ umbrella.

3. Every person should be careful about _____ use of detergents.

4. Any man who wants _____ supper hot had better come and get it.

5. One of the men spent half _____ pay on a lottery ticket.

6. One of the wives made _____ husband 17 pancakes.

7. Nobody cut _____ hair.

8. Somebody had better move _____ car out of my driveway.

9. Each woman made _____ own sandwich.

Try It in a Paragraph

Read the story below. Decide whether or not each underlined word is used correctly. If one is not correct, choose the correct word from the choices lettered (a) to (d) on the right. Choice (a) is always the same as the underlined word in the story.

It was midnight, and Bill and <u>its</u>¹ wife were snoring soundly in <u>there</u>² room above the pawnshop.

1. (a)| |its
   (b)| |their
   (c)| |her
   (d)| |his

2. (a)| |there
   (b)| |their
   (c)| |theirs
   (d)| |hers

One of <u>her</u>³ arms dangled off the side of the bed. His arms were wrapped around <u>hisself</u>⁴.

3. (a)| |her
   (b)| |hers
   (c)| |its
   (d)| |my

4. (a)| |hisself
   (b)| |himself
   (c)| |his
   (d)| |hers

Suddenly he awoke. Someone was banging <u>their</u>⁵ fists on the door below.

5. (a)| |their
   (b)| |its
   (c)| |his
   (d)| |her

6
<u>Bill's</u> wife sat up in bed.

6. (a)|| Bill's

(b)|| Bills'

(c)|| Billes

(d)|| Bills

7
"Is that <u>ours</u> door?" she mumbled, still half asleep.
Bill nodded and put his head out the window.

7. (a)|| ours

(b)|| its

(c)|| his

(d)| our

8
"Come down here," demanded a <u>mans'</u> voice.

8. (a)|| mans'

(b)|| mens'

(c)| men's

(d)|| man's

"At this hour?" said Bill angrily.

9
"Come down or I'll break <u>youre</u> door in," said the voice
from below.

9. (a)|| youre

(b)|| your

(c)|| your's

(d)|| yours

Grumbling to himself, Bill stumbled down the stairs
10
from <u>their's</u> room. "What is it?" he asked.

"What time is it?" said the caller.

"What!" said Bill. "You wake me up in the middle of
the night and ask me the time?"

10. (a)|| theirs

(b)|| there

(c)|| their

(d)|| their's

11
"Well," answered the man, "you've got <u>mine</u> watch,
haven't you?"

11. (a)|| mine

(b)|| my

(c)|| myself

(d)| my's

15. THE CASE OF THE MISSING LETTER (CONTRACTIONS)

The apostrophe (') has two very important uses:

1. To show belonging or possession, as in the man's knife. [You learned about this in the last chapter.]

2. To show that a letter or letters are missing from a word: can't, it's, there's.

Like all other punctuation marks, the apostrophe (') helps make printed words more like spoken words. You often take short cuts when you speak and make two words into one. Instead of saying are not, you leave out the o in not and say aren't. Instead of saying they are, you say they're. And for it is, you say it's. When these words are written, the apostrophe is used to show where the letter is missing. Two words that are said and written as one are called CONTRACTIONS. Here are some common contractions:

LEARNING GOALS:

- To learn how to form contractions

- To learn when to use don't and when to use doesn't

1. These contractions are made from a pronoun and the word is. The letter i is left out to make the contractions, and the apostrophe shows where it is left out.

> he is = he's
> it is = it's
> who is = who's

2. These contractions are made from a verb and the word not. The letter o in not is left out to make the contractions, and the apostrophe shows where it is left out.

does not = doesn't	is not = isn't
do not = don't	was not = wasn't
has not = hasn't	could not = couldn't
have not = haven't	cannot = can't

(You can see that in the contraction can't, one n has been left out as well as the o.)

3. These contractions are made from a verb and a pronoun. To make the contraction, the first one or two letters of the verb are left

out. The apostrophe marks the spot where the letter or letters are left out.

I will = I'll	they are = they're
I have = I've	you are = you're
she has = she's	we are = we're
he has = he's	

You can see that a few contractions have more than one meaning. For example, she's can mean she is or she has; and he's can mean he is or he has. You can tell which meaning the contraction has by seeing it in a sentence:

> She's my girlfriend.
> She is my girlfriend.

> She's left me.
> She has left me.

Some contractions might give you trouble because they look and sound like other words. These other words show belonging or possession for the pronouns it, who, and they.

It's, for example, is the contraction of it is. Its without the apostrophe shows possession for it.

> It's time for your medicine.
> It's never too late.

> The horse lost its rider.
> The dog lost its collar.

They're is the contraction of they are. Their shows possession for they.

> They're here.
> They're cool.

> Their sandwiches are cheap.
> Their telephones aren't working.

Who's is the contraction of who is. Whose shows possession for who.

> Who's there?
> Who's going?

> Whose coffee is this?
> Whose car should we take?

Try It

Underline the contractions in the paragraph below.

> The bright southern California sun refracts through the glass-bottle walls, filling the house with amber, green and blue lights. "When I look around and see what I've done, I don't know how I did it," says Tressa Prisbrey, the 82-year-old creator of Grandma Prisbrey's Bottle Village. "I built it all myself. Built the houses, put the cement in, mixed it. That's quite a job for an old woman."

Try It

Put an apostrophe wherever it is needed in the following sentences.

1. "Whos there?" a man called.
2. Theyre certainly not going to eat again after that big dinner, are they?
3. Its the time of year when the trees lose their leaves.
4. Its collar is gone.
5. Its the revolution.

Try It Again

Fill each blank in the sentences below with a word that shows possession or with a contraction. Use the words in parentheses as guides.

1. (The men) _____ hats are not here.
2. (The women) _____ on a high-protein diet.
3. (The weather) _____ going to rain.
4. (Who) _____ making so much noise?
5. Don't be afraid. Even though (it) _____ growling, (it) _____ tail is wagging.
6. I don't know (who) _____ house this is.

USING DON'T AND DOESN'T

The contractions don't and doesn't are likely to cause trouble if you aren't careful when you use them.

You use doesn't instead of don't with he, she, or it:

Wrong	Right
He don't smoke.	He doesn't smoke.
She don't cook.	She doesn't cook.
It don't work.	It doesn't work.

You use <u>don't</u> with <u>I</u>, <u>you</u>, <u>we</u>, or <u>they</u>:

They don't like it.
You don't want it.
We don't have it.
I don't care.

Try It

Put <u>doesn't</u> or <u>don't</u> in each blank below.

1. It _____ look right.

2. I _____ like it.

3. It _____ appeal to me.

4. You _____ look very tired.

5. He _____ feel well.

6. It _____ matter.

7. That _____ sound right.

8. Fred _____ have enough time.

9. The women _____ usually drink tea.

10. My wife and I _____ know how to get there.

Try It in a Paragraph

Read each of the two stories below. Decide whether or not each under-lined word is used correctly. If one is not correct, choose the correct answer from the choices lettered (a) to (d). Blacken the space next to your choice. Choice (a) is always the same as the underlined word in the story.

STORY 1:

1
"<u>Whose</u> next?" the nurse asked.

1. (a) | | Whose

    (b) | | Who's

(c)| | Whoose

(d)| | Who'se

A nervous-looking man got up and walked into the

doctor's office. He told the doctor that he was so

worried about making a speech that he had butter-

2

flies in <u>his</u>' stomach.

3

"<u>Its</u> terrible," the man said.

4

"I <u>cann't</u> eat or sleep."

"Take an aspirin," said the doctor. "The butterflies will

5

go away, and <u>your</u> stomach will feel fine.

The man moaned and said, "But I took an aspirin, and

6

<u>their</u> playing ping-pong with it."

STORY 2:

"Judge," complains an angry lady to the court, "this

1

husband of mine <u>don't</u> save his money."

2. (a)| | his'

(b)| | hi's

(c)| | his

(d)| | he is

3. (a)| | Its

(b)| | It's

(c)| | Its'

(d)| | I'ts

4. (a)| | cann't

(b)| | cant'

(c)| | can't

(d)| | cant

5. (a)| | your

(b)| | you're

(c)| | you'r

(d)| | you

6. (a)| | their

(b)| | there

(c)| | the'ir

(d)| | they're

1. (a)| | don't

(b)| | do'nt

(c) || doesn't

(d) || do

"Yes, sir, I <u>doesn't</u> deny it," the man says.
2

2. (a) || doesn't

(b) || do

(c) || don't

(d) || did

"But my wife <u>doesn't</u> treat me right. Why, if I pawn the
3
kitchen stove to get a little money, she <u>don't</u> miss it
4
for two weeks."

3. (a) || doesn't

(b) || don't

(c) || did

(d) || do

4. (a) || don't

(b) || do

(c) || did

(d) || doesn't

16. NO + NO = YES (DOUBLE NEGATIVES)

Sentences that have two "no" words in them are incorrect.

EUGENE: "I don't know nothing."

VALERIE: "Well, if you don't know nothing,
you must know something."

Eugene's sentence is incorrect, but think about the two sentences above. You can see that two "no" words seem to make a "yes." Eugene should have said, "I don't know anything." Then there would be only one word meaning "no" in his sentence The word is <u>don't</u>. Sentences should have only one "no" in them.

The following words mean "no":

no	hardly
never	scarcely
none	

If you use one of these words in a sentence, you must be careful not to use another "no" word.

LEARNING GOALS:

- To recognize a double negative

- To write sentences that contain only one "no" word

Wrong	Right
I don't have no money.	I don't have any money.
	(or) I have no money.
I don't never go bowling.	I don't ever go bowling.
	(or) I never go bowling.
I couldn't find none.	I couldn't find any.
	(or) I could find none.
I don't scarcely know him.	I scarcely know him.
He doesn't hardly talk.	He hardly talks.

The word scarcely or hardly is used alone in a sentence.
   All the words that start with the letters no- mean "no," too:

> nobody
>
> nothing
>
> nowhere

If you are writing or saying a sentence that already has a "no" in it, you do not use those "no" words. You use a word that begins with any- instead:

> anybody
>
> anything
>
> anywhere
>
> I don't know anybody here.
>
> We're not going anywhere tonight.

Words that end with not or -n't mean "no," also:

have not	didn't
can't	does not
isn't	don't

Here are some sentences that use these words correctly:

> I have not given her any presents.
>
> I can't do any better.
>
> Don't ever give me any trouble.

Try It

Change each sentence below so that it has only one "no" word in it.
   1. There isn't no time left.
   2. I can't hardly believe her.

3. You haven't no right to do that.
4. I couldn't find none.
5. They didn't win no games.
6. It wasn't hardly worth the trouble.
7. I haven't no excuse.
8. There isn't no time to fool around.
9. I don't have nothing to lose.
10. He doesn't trust nobody.

Try It in a Paragraph

Read the story below. Decide whether or not each underlined group of words is used correctly. If a group is not correct, choose the correct words from the choices lettered (a) to (d) on the right. Blacken the space next to your letter choice. Choice (a) is always the same as the underlined words in the story.

1. A man walked into a doctor's office and said, "Doctor, I can't hardly do anything. I feel terrible."

1. (a)| | I can't hardly do anything.
   (b)| | I can't hardly do nothing.
   (c)| | I can't do nothing.
   (d)| | I can hardly do anything.

2. Let me ask you a few questions," said the doctor. "Do you drink much liquor?"

"Oh, no," said the man. "I don't drink no liquor."

2. (a)| | "I don't drink no liquor."
   (b)| | "I don't drink any liquor."
   (c)| | "I don't drink hardly any liquor."
   (d)| | "I don't drink none."

3. "Do you smoke?" asked the doctor.

"No," said the man. "<u>It isn't hardly worth the money.</u>"

3. (a)|| "It isn't hardly worth the money."

   (b)|| "It isn't hardly worth no money."

   (c)|| "It isn't hardly worth any money."

   (d)|| "It is hardly worth the money."

4. "Do you run around much at night?" the doctor asked.

"<u>There isn't no time</u> to fool around," answered the man.

4. (a)|| "There isn't no time

   (b)|| "There isn't any time

   (c)|| "There isn't scarcely time

   (d)|| "There's not hardly time

5. "<u>I don't do nothing</u> like that. I'm in bed by ten o'clock for a good night's rest."

5. (a)|| "I don't do nothing

   (b)|| "I don't do none

   (c)|| "I don't do anything

   (d)|| "I do anything

6. "Tell me," the doctor said, "do you have sharp pains in the head?"

"Yes, <u>I can't scarcely understand it</u>, but I do," the man replied.

"That's your trouble, my dear man," the doctor said. "Your halo is on too tight."

6. (a)||I can't scarcely understand it,

   (b)||I can't hardly understand it,

   (c)||I can't do nothing to understand it,

   (d)||I can scarcely understand it,

17. WORDS THAT CAUSE TROUBLE

Some words are often confused with other words that sound or look like them or that are used in almost the same way. They are common words that are used every day, but people seem to mix them up. This chapter will help you use these troublesome words correctly.

LEARNING GOALS:

• To distinquish between: lay and lie; between and among; beside and besides; farther and further; and like and as

• To use different from, could have, is, kind of, sort of, and try to

LAY AND LIE

Lay means "put" or "place" something down. The two forms of lay that show past action are laid and have laid or had laid. Lie means "rest" or "stay in a flat position." The two forms of lie that show past action are lay and have lain or had lain.

Lay your book on the table.
I laid mine there as soon as I came in yesterday.
It has lain there ever since.
Every night he lays his mattress down and lies on it.

BETWEEN AND AMONG

Between is used when you are talking about only two things. Among is used when you talk about more than two things.

Three robbers were resting after a holdup. One robber leaned over and whispered to one of the others, "Listen, just between the two of us, I don't want to split this money among the three of us."

BESIDE AND BESIDES

Beside means "by the side of" or "at the side of." Besides means "in addition to" or "moreover."

Besides driving through the red light, she parked beside a fire hydrant.

113

DIFFERENT FROM, NOT DIFFERENT THAN

Use different from when you compare things.

> Summer is as different from winter as honey is from vinegar.

> This car is different from mine.

COULD HAVE, NOT COULD OF

Always use could have.

> His soles were so thin, he could have stepped on a dime and told if it were heads or tails.

> I could have cried when I heard the news.

FARTHER AND FURTHER

Farther has the small word far in it. This might help you remember that farther is used when you mean distance as counted in miles or blocks. Further means "more," or "to a greater degree."

> Chicago is farther west than Philadelphia.

> "Do you have further plans for me?" John asked his boss.

IS, NOT IS WHEN OR IS WHERE

When you define something, that is, when you tell what it is, use only is.

Wrong: Misery is when you don't have the exact change to get on the last bus home.

Right: Misery is not having the exact change to get on the last bus home.

KIND OF AND SORT OF,
NOT KIND OF A AND SORT OF A

Don't use a after kind of or sort of.

> What kind of hot dogs do you serve here?
> What sort of restaurant is this anyway?

LIKE AND AS

"Charleen looks beautiful, like a model should." This sentence may sound all right to your ear, but you probably know that it is wrong. The sentence should be, "Charleen looks beautiful, as a model should." Like can only be followed by a noun or a pronoun, not a noun and a verb. Like before the words "a model should" is wrong. "A model should" has both a noun, model, and a verb, should, in it.

Wrong: That car looks like it's going to fall apart.
Right: That car looks as if it's going to fall apart.

Wrong: Do like I do.
Right: Do as I do.
Right: She cooks like an expert.
Right: He sounds like a nice person.

In the last two sentences, like is followed by a noun only.

TRY TO NOT TRY AND

Wrong: I will try and come.
Right: I will try to come.

Try It

Find the troublesome words in each sentence below. If they are used incorcorectly, change them.

1. How much further do we have to go before I can take his blindfold off?
2. Why didn't you tell me before that the car didn't work? I could of gone with Joe.
3. Don't try to start trouble among the two of us.
4. How much different than that can you get?
5. She walks as a movie star.

6. What kind of a friend are you?
7. Lay down for a while.
8. You sound just like my wife.
9. Try and help her get her car started.
10. She was standing beside her husband when she fainted.

CHECKUP TEST 3

Possessives

LEARNING GOALS:

• To review Chapters 14-17

1. Underline the words in the sentences below that show posssession.

   a. It is Robert's car.
   b. It is his car.
   c. The peacocks' feathers were brightly colored.
   d. My aunt's house is large.
   e. This is the lady whose book I borrowed.

2. Put an apostrophe (') where needed in the sentences below.

   a. Johns favorite programs are on today.
   b. The Norwegians scenery is beautiful.
   c. Your words make no sense.
   d. Keep the dogs collars loose.
   e. My eyes are closed.

3. In each sentence, write the pronoun that shows possession.

   a. I have finished _____ dinner.
   b. We will do _____ work later.
   c. _____ books are these?
   d. I know you are doing _____ best.
   e. He helped the man _____ car broke down.

4. Underline the correct pronouns in each sentence.

   a. Everybody has (his or her, their) own umbrella.
   b. Nobody has (his or her, their) own raincoat.
   c. Each man does (his, their) own thing.
   d. One of the women had (her, their) own pencil.
   e. Somebody left (his or her, their) hat here.

The Case of the Missing Letter (Contractions)

5. Put the apostrophe in the proper place in the words below.

   a. cant
   b. wouldnt
   c. youre
   d. havent
   e. Im

6. Write the contractions for the words below.

    a. _____ he is
    b. _____ does not
    c. _____ I will
    d. _____ it is
    e. _____ who is
    f. _____ has not
    g. _____ I have
    h. _____ they are
    i. _____ do not
    j. _____ could not

7. Write doesn't or don't in each blank below.

    a. He _____ even know my name.
    b. I _____ know his, either.
    c. Mr. and Mrs. Gray _____ often visit us.
    d. Judy _____ want to wait.
    e. _____ Mary Ellen have a dog?

No + No = Yes (Double Negatives)

8. On the lines below, rewrite any sentences that are incorrect.

    a. Boris doesn't like anybody.

    _____

    b. He don't know nobody.

    _____

    c. I don't have no time right now.

    _____

    d. I hardly ever do.

    _____

    e. There isn't much food in the refrigerator.

    _____

    f. There isn't hardly any left.

    _____

    g. There's no sun today.

    _____

    h. Henry hasn't no umbrella.

    _____

    i. It doesn't seem to matter.

    _____

    j. I cannot do nothing about it.

    _____

Words that Cause Trouble

9. Put <u>X</u> beside any sentence that is incorrect.

a. _____ James laid down on the couch.
b. _____ I could of cried when I saw you.
c. _____ Janie's sister looks a lot like her.
d. _____ Happiness is when you take a day off.
e. _____ What sort of a place do you have?

10. Underline the correct word or words in the parentheses.

a. (Lie, Lay) down on the couch.
b. (Lie, Lay) your bag down and stay awhile.
c. Bernie hasn't got the time to go. (Beside, Besides), he hasn't got the money.
d. The rich are different (from, than) you and me.
e. I have traveled (farther, further) south than you have.
f. You look (like, as if) you've had a rough day.
g. You look (like, as) my cousin.
h. He was (beside, besides) himself with anger.
i. That's a secret (between, among) you and me.
j. That's a secret (between, among) you, me, and the lamp-post.
k. Helen said she could (have, of) stayed forever.
l. Before you say anything (farther, further), remember what you promised.
m. Love is (when you don't say, not saying) you're sorry.
n. That woman is some (kind of, kind of a) pest.
o. Try (to, and) do it.

18. PERIODS, QUESTION MARKS, AND EXCLAMATION POINTS

Courtesy of *The New York Times*

LEARNING GOALS:

• To learn when to use periods, question marks, and exclamation points

There are three kinds of marks that are used after sentences to help you understand what is being said or written. They show how your voice rises and falls when you speak.

Read these sentences aloud and listen to yourself:

> I found it!
>
> What did you say?
>
> Oh, nothing.

Your voice probably went down with a bang after "I found it!" It probably rose after "What did you say?" And it probably paused after "Oh," then said "nothing" and went down and stopped. Would you have read those sentences the same way even without the marks? Maybe you would have. But look at the different ways these PUNCTUATION MARKS tell you how to read the sentences on the next page.

120

Oh, yeah.

Oh, yeah!

Oh, yeah?

Your voice should have changed at the end of each sentence above. The PERIOD (.) told you to drop your voice and stop. The EXCLAMATION POINT (!) told you to read the words with excitement or surprise. You might have said "Oh, yeah!" in answer to the question, "Would you like twenty-five dollars?" The QUESTION MARK (?) told you to raise your voice at the end. "Oh, yeah?" could sound like the opening sentence to a fight.

Periods, question marks, and exclamation points are the punctuation marks that end sentences.

The period is used when you say or tell something.

The question mark is used when you ask a question.

The exclamation point is used when you shout or say something in anger, excitement, or surprise.

Try It

End each sentence below with a period, a question mark, or an exclamation point.

1. Watch out
2. How do you say "horse" in Spanish
3. Don't you ever take a vacation
4. Yes, I do
5. What's happening
6. Help
7. Will I see you again
8. Fire
9. That'll be seventy cents for two pieces of pizza
10. Great

Try It in a Paragraph

Put the correct punctuation mark at the end of each sentence in the stories below.

STORY 1:

An excited young man ran frantically down the boat

dock__
    1

He leaped across a strip of water and landed with a crash on the deck of the boat__2

"Well," he cried, as he picked himself up, "I made it__3"

"What's your hurry__4" asked a deck hand. "The boat is coming in."

STORY 2:

"Do you find that advertising brings quick results__5"

"Yes, indeed__6 Why only the other day we advertised for a night watchman, and that very night the safe was robbed__7"

19. COMMAS

There are many uses for the punctuation mark called a COMMA. Read this story:

LEARNING GOALS:

• To use commas in a series

• To use commas before and, but, or, and for

> A man's car stalled at the corner, and the traffic light turned red, yellow, and green. A policeman stepped up beside his car and asked, "What's the matter, mister? Haven't we got any colors you like?"

There are five commas in the three sentences above. As you can see from the story, they are used in different ways.

COMMAS IN A SERIES

A series is three or more words or group of words written one after another. Commas are used to separate words or groups of words in a series. Look at this sentence:

> I like pizza hot dogs potato chips ice cream sodas and fried onions.

Without commas, the sentence above is unclear. Do you like ice cream sodas or ice cream and sodas?

With commas, it is easy to understand what you like.

> I like pizza, hot dogs, potato chips, ice cream, sodas, and fried onions.

Notice that a comma is put after each thing in the series and also before and.

A series may also have nouns and hooking words that help describe the nouns:

> He sent her a bottle of perfume, a bouquet of roses, and the bill for his damaged car.

123

A series may have verbs in it instead of nouns:

He coughed, sneezed, and blew his nose.

Or a series may use hooking words that describe nouns or verbs. The hooking words below tell where they looked:

They looked under the bed, on top of the
refrigerator, and in the closet.

In all the sentences above, there was a comma after each thing in the series and before <u>and</u>. There is another way to write a series without using commas. You can join all the words or groups of words with <u>and</u>:

He winked and smiled and walked toward her.
She saw him and frowned and turned away.

Usually it is easier and quicker to use commas and only one <u>and</u>.

Another way the comma is used is to separate two or more words that describe a noun and that come before it. The noun is underlined in the two sentences below.

The dreary, ugly <u>street</u> was lined with
uncollected garbage.

He wrote a long, angry <u>letter</u> to the mayor.

Try It

Put commas where they are needed in the following sentences. Some of the sentences don't need commas.

1. Bob Carol Ted and Alice were in a movie.
2. They ordered tomato soup pork chops and coffee.
3. The house smelled of fried chicken and fresh coffee.
4. The man's loud angry words sounded like Chinese slang.
5. He took off his hat threw it on the table turned on the television set and dropped into an easy chair.
6. She jumped out of her car waved her fist in the air and yelled at the careless driver.
7. The bullet bounced off a tree hit a rock and knocked over the beer can.

8. We chased them through the streets down back alleys up fire escapes and over rooftops.

9. Stop yelling and crying and stamping your feet.

10. His old worn shoes have thin soles.

COMMAS BEFORE <u>AND</u>, <u>BUT</u>, <u>OR</u>, AND <u>FOR</u>

Sometimes two sentences are joined together to make one longer sentence. This is usually done to make writing more interesting to read. The words that connect the two sentences to make them into one are <u>and</u>, <u>but</u>, <u>or</u>, and <u>for</u>. A comma is used before these small connecting words.

Here are some examples in this story about two old friends:

The bar was filled with smoke, <u>and</u> in a corner sat two old friends.

They had not been drinking very long, <u>but</u> they were already quite drunk.

They finally left the bar, <u>for</u> it was getting late.

Outside, one drunk asked the other, "Is that the sun up there, <u>or</u> is it still the moon?"

"I don't know," said the other. "I don't live around here."

You can see that without the commas, the long sentences would be too long to read without stopping to take a breath. Commas here mark the spot where you should pause before reading on.

Short sentences connected with <u>and</u>, <u>but</u>, <u>or</u>, or <u>for</u> usually don't need commas. Here are some examples:

She liked it but I didn't.
He'll go or I will.
Run over and get it.

Try It

Put commas where they are needed in the sentences below.

1. The room was dim and in a corner sat a boy and girl.

2. They had not been engaged very long but his love was already beginning to cool.

3. He laughed and I asked him what he knew about her.

4. The tray tilted and the dishes fell.

5. He turned the bottle upside down, but only a drop of water trickled out.

6. He started to run for he was sure a man was following him.

7. They ordered another pizza for they still had an hour before Angelo's closed.

8. They could cross the picket line or they could look for work at another factory.

9. He tried but she didn't.

Try It in a Paragraph

Read the story below. Decide whether or not each underlined part of the sentence is correct. If a part is not correct, choose the correct words from the choices (a) to (d) at the right. Blacken the space next to your choice. Choice (a) is always the same as the underlined part of the story.

1. It was <u>a busy crowded Saturday</u> afternoon.

   1. (a)| | a busy crowded Saturday

   (b)| | a busy crowded, Saturday

   (c)| | a, busy, crowded Saturday

   (d)| | a busy, crowded Saturday

2. The sidewalks were filled <u>with shoppers, and cars moved</u> bumper to bumper along the streets.

   2. (a)| | with shoppers, and cars moved

   (b)| | with shoppers and cars moved

   (c)| | with shoppers, and, cars moved

   (d)| | with shoppers and cars, moved

3. At a crowded street corner, a line of cars waited for the light to change. The light <u>turned, green but, the cars</u> didn't move.

3. (a) | | turned, green but, the cars

(b) | | turned green but, the cars

(c) | | turned green, but the cars

(d) | | turned green but the cars

4. The first car in line had stalled. The driver of the stalled car was clearly nervous. He quickly <u>got out of his car, opened the hood and</u> worked with the engine.

4. (a) | | got out of his car, opened the hood and

(b) | | got out of his car opened the hood, and

(c) | | got out of his car opened the hood and

(d) | | got out of his car, opened the hood, and

5. He was <u>upset and angry,</u> for the driver of the car behind him had begun honking his horn.

5. (a) | | upset and angry, for

(b) | | upset and angry for

(c) | | upset and, angry for

(d) | | upset, and angry, for

6. It was plain the driver couldn't get his car <u>started</u>

   <u>but, the man</u> behind him didn't let up on his horn.

6. (a)| | started but, the man

   (b)| |, started but, the

   man

   (c)| | started but the man,

   (d)| | started, but the man

7. Finally, the driver of the stalled car stopped <u>work-</u>

   <u>ing on his engine, looked up and walked</u> over to

   the honker.

7. (a)| | working on his

   engine, looked up

   and walked

   (b)| | working on his

   engine, looked up,

   and walked

   (c)| | working on his

   engine looked up

   and walked

   (d)| | working, on his

   engine, looked up

   and, walked

"If you will fix my car," he said calmly, "I'll be glad

to keep blowing your horn for you."

20. COMMAS FOR INTERRUPTERS

Courtesy of General Foods

Words that break up or interrupt the main idea of a sentence are called interrupters. Read the sentence below and watch how the underlined words interrupt the important words in the sentence.

He turned back, <u>of course</u>, because he was afraid.

The important words in the sentence are <u>He turned back because he was afraid</u>. The words <u>of course</u> are extra words that are not really needed for the meaning of the sentence. Words like this are called interrupters. <u>Of course</u> is separated from the other words by commas. The commas make the sentence easier to read.

Here are some more examples of interrupters. The interrupters are underlined.

He tried, <u>however</u>, to get her to stay.
The water, <u>therefore</u>, was cold.
<u>In fact</u>, they said we shouldn't even try to catch
    them.

As you can see from the third example above, an interrupter can be used at the beginning of a sentence, too.

Sometimes a word like <u>well</u>, <u>why</u>, <u>no</u>, or <u>oh</u> begins a sentence. It, too, is followed by a comma:

> <u>Well</u>, that's that.
> <u>Why</u>, yes I do.
> <u>Oh</u>, do you eat flowers, too?

The following sentences show another kind of interrupter:

> If that's all, <u>sir</u>, I'll show you to the door.
> Please come here, <u>Judy</u>.
> Well, <u>Mom</u>, we'll see you soon.

These interrupters tell who is being spoken to in a sentence. This kind of interrupter is also set off by commas, or by one comma if it is at the end of a sentence. The last sentence above has two interrupters, <u>Well</u> and <u>Mom</u>. They are both set off by commas.

One way to tell whether words are interrupters is by crossing them out of the sentence. If the meaning of the sentence is still clear, the crossed-out words are interrupters. They should be separated from the other words in the sentence by two commas, one before and one after.

Try It

Put commas wherever they are needed in the sentences below.

1. No Mary that's not the way to do it.
2. Why I know how.
3. Frank however does not pay back the money he borrows.
4. The men in fact know nothing about the strike.
5. The kitchen sink is still leaking however.
6. Oh he didn't.
7. Man I don't want to go through that again.
8. He too said he was hungry.
9. Yes please let me try.
10. I know what's going on I think.

MORE ABOUT INTERRUPTERS

One of the most important kinds of interrupters is a group of words that follow right after a noun. These words tell you something more about the noun.

My husband, <u>a carpenter</u>, is on strike.

The words <u>a carpenter</u> tell you something more about <u>my husband</u>. Two commas, one before and one after, separate <u>a carpenter</u> from the other words in the sentence. You can test whether <u>a carpenter</u> is an interrupter if the rest of the sentence still makes sense. The sentence, "My husband is on strike," makes sense by itself.

Here are some more examples of interrupters that describe the noun they follow.

That is Mrs. Maslow, <u>my landlady</u>.
My car, <u>an old Buick</u>, broke down on the freeway.
That man, <u>the one on the motorcycle</u>, is my brother.
The puppy, <u>cold and scared</u>, came home.

Try It

Put commas wherever they are needed in the sentences below.

1. The jaywalker a well-dressed old man shook his umbrella at the policeman who gave him a ticket.
2. A toothbrush worn and limp was the only thing he carried when he hitchhiked.
3. The pickle sour as a lemon made her mouth pucker.
4. Fourteen couples dancing close packed the small living room.
5. People screaming and crying climbed onto chairs and tables.
6. Sonny who wrote advertisements for a living had an idea for making big money.
7. The entertainers out for some fun after their own places had closed all went to Valentino's until 4 A.M.
8. José dressed in a yellow silk shirt and white trousers danced every night at the Hombre Cafe.
9. An elderly Cuban lady the owner of a beauty parlor called el Olé called the people of East 100th Street to a block meeting.
10. He banged the bottom of the catsup bottle now almost empty.

Try It in a Paragraph

Read the story on the next page. Decide whether or not each underlined part of the sentence is correct. If it is not, choose the correct words from the choices lettered (a) to (d) on the right. Blacken the space next to your choice. Choice (a) is always the same as the underlined part in the story.

1
A man, <u>hot and thirsty</u> walked up to a refreshment stand.

He asked for a soda with a dash of horseradish. The
2
counterman, <u>a bored-looking man</u> prepared it and
3
handed it to him. The counterman, <u>of course</u>, was used to strange requests.

4
The soda <u>cold and foamy</u>, did not last long.

5
The man, <u>drank it</u>, and smacked his lips.

6
The man, <u>leaning over the counter</u> said to the
7
counterman, "You think it strange <u>I suppose</u> that I should come in here and ask for a soda with horse-radish in it."

1. (a)| |, hot and thirsty

   (b)| |, hot and thirsty,

   (c)| | hot and thirsty,

   (d)| | hot and thirsty

2. (a)| |, a bored-looking man

   (b)| | a bored-looking man

   (c)| |, a bored-looking man,

   (d)| | a bored-looking man,

3. (a)| |, of course,

   (b)| | of course

   (c)| |, of course

   (d)| | of course,

4. (a)| | cold and foamy,

   (b)| | cold and foamy

   (c)| |, cold and foamy,

   (d)| |, cold and foamy

5. (a)| |, drank it,

   (b)| | drank it,

   (c)| |, drank it

   (d)| | drank it

6. (a)| |, leaning over the counter

   (b)| |, leaning, over the counter

(c)| | leaning over the
    counter,

(d)| |, leaning over the
    counter,

7. (a)| | I suppose

(b)| |, I suppose,

(c)| |, I suppose

(d)| | I, suppose

8

"Oh, no," said the counterman, "I like it with catsup

myself."

8. (a)| | "Oh, no,"

(b)| | "Oh no,"

(c)| | "Oh no"

(d)| | "Oh no,

21. COMMAS IN DATES AND PLACES

LEARNING GOALS:

- To use commas correctly in dates

- To use commas correctly in place names

COMMAS IN DATES

Commas are used in dates to separate the numbers and make the dates easy to read. In a date, a comma always separates the day from the year, or the month from the year.

> December 25, 1971
> January 1, 1943
> A shot was "heard around the world" in April, 1775.
> The Reverend Martin Luther King, Jr., was born in January, 1929.

Try It

Put commas where they are needed in the following sentences.

1. The grape pickers' first union meeting was held in California in September 1962.

2. Malcolm X was born on May 19 1925.

3. The Mexican Revolution began in 1910.

4. On May 17 1954 the Supreme Court ordered that black and white children attend the same schools.

5. The Declaration of Independence was signed on July 4 1776.

COMMAS IN NAMES OF PLACES

Commas are used to separate the name of a city from the name of a state. When you write your address, you should place a comma between city and state:

> Mr. Willie Gordon
> 1356 Wasdale Avenue
> Newark, New Jersey

When you are writing a sentence and need to use the name of a city and state, use a comma to separate the city from the state and also place a comma after the state unless it comes at the end of a sentence:

Sidney lives at 1846 50th Street, Brooklyn, New York, but he plans to move to Kansas City, Missouri, after his vacation.

I live in Chicago, Illinois.

Try It

Place commas in the sentences below to separate the names of cities from the names of states.

1. The St. Louis Cardinals have a new stadium in St. Louis Missouri.
2. If the fan breaks, the directions say to send it back to the manufacturer in Birmingham Alabama for a complete refund.
3. Don't forget to send an invitation to Aunt Annie in San Jose California or to Uncle James in Pittsburgh Pennsylvania.
4. Next year we plan to stop in Dayton Ohio and Wheeling West Virginia on our way to see Mr. and Mrs. Simpson in Jacksonville Florida.

Try It in a Letter

Read the business letter below. Place commas where they are necessary.

84 South Street
Elmsford New York 10501
July 1 1979

Credit Department
Tiffany & Co.
727 Fifth Avenue
New York New York 10022

Dear Credit Department:

I would like to open a charge account at your store. I live at the above address and I work at Phraney's Drugstore in Tarrytown New York. I have charge accounts at Bloomingdale's Saks and Macy's. I have bank accounts at Chase Manhattan and the Bank of New York in Elmsford.

Please send me an application.

Yours truly,

Kenneth R. Sczyan

Try It in a Paragraph

Read the story below. Decide whether or not each underlined part of the sentence is correct. If it is not, choose the correct answer from the list of choices on the right. Blacken the space next to your choice. Choice (a) is always the same as that in the story.

Two prisoners at Sing Sing State Prison at <u>Ossining</u>¹ <u>New York,</u> were busily working together one day.

1. (a) | | Ossining New York,
   (b) | | Ossining, New York,
   (c) | | Ossining New, York
   (d) | | Ossining New York

The older of the two men had been behind bars since <u>February 14, 1947,</u>² when he was convicted of shooting a man in <u>Buffalo New York.</u>³

2. (a) | | February 14, 1947,
   (b) | | February 14, 1947
   (c) | | February 14 1947
   (d) | | February, 14 1947

3. (a) | | Buffalo New York.
   (b) | | Buffalo, New, York
   (c) | | Buffalo New, York.
   (d) | | Buffalo, New, York.

The younger man had been in prison since <u>March 3,</u>⁴ <u>1977</u>⁵ for writing bad checks in <u>Albany, New York.</u>

4. (a) | | March 3, 1977
   (b) | | March 3, 1977,
   (c) | | March, 3, 1977
   (d) | | March 3 1977,

5. (a) | | Albany, New York.
   (b) | | Albany, New, York.
   (c) | | Albany New York.
   (d) | | Albany New, York.

Suddenly the two men who had been working so well together started fighting. After they had been separated, the guard asked what had caused the fight, the

6

worst he had seen since taking the job on <u>June, 11,</u>

<u>1966</u>.

Still struggling to get free, the younger prisoner yelled,

"He called me a dirty number."

6. (a) | | June, 11, 1966.

(b) | | June 11, 1966.

(c) | | June 11 1966.

(d) | | June, 11 1966.

22. QUOTATION MARKS

LEARNING GOALS:

- **To learn when to use quotation marks**

- **To learn how to use other punctuation with quotation marks**

QUOTATION MARKS (" ") are put around words that tell, or quote, exactly what a person said:

> "May I help you?" the saleswoman asked.
> "We won't go!" the students shouted.
> "I love you," he whispered.

In the first sentence, the saleswoman is asking a question. The words she says have quotation marks around them. Because her words ask a question, a question mark (?) is at the end of them. Notice that the question mark is inside the quotation marks. There is a period (.) at the end of the whole sentence.

In the second sentence, an exclamation point (!) is at the end of the words the students shouted. Notice again that the exclamation point is inside the quotation marks, and a period is at the end of the sentence.

In the third sentence, a comma with the quotation marks following is put after the words the man whispered. This sentence also ends with a period.

Try It

Put quotation marks and a period in the correct places in the following sentences.

1. The movie was nothing great, he said
2. You'll go to that school and like it fine, she said
3. You've heard? we asked
4. You don't mean that! I cried
5. They're in the gas station talking or in the club playing pool, the man shouted out the window

When the quotation marks are at the end of the sentence, a comma is always before the beginning of the quoted words. The sentence ends with the punctuation mark that fits the tone of the spoken words. Notice that the punctuation mark at the end of the sentence is inside the quotation marks.

> He said angrily, "Get out of here!"
> The boy asked, "Why doesn't he let her stay?"
> She answered softly, "But I don't want to go."

Try It

Put quotation marks and a comma in the correct places in the following sentences.

1. He shouted They've landed!
2. The policeman asked the driver Where's your license?
3. She picked the petals from the flowers as she said He loves me; he loves me not.
4. The mother asked her son Where's the dog?
5. In a low voice he said Yeah, we mean get out.

Try It Again

Put quotation marks and a comma in the correct places in the following paragraphs.

About 200 grade-school children from the Harlem community marveled at the soccer wizardry of Pelé yesterday at a clinic designed to foster interest in the sport and encourage the area's youngsters to stay in school and earn a degree.

Soccer is an easy sport to understand. Kids can catch on to it easily Pelé said before making his entrance at the cavernous armory. And it's not an expensive sport; it requires very little equipment.

As Pelé and his friends worked with the children in groups of four and five, teaching ball control and passing, a member of the clinic staff said We don't have enough concerned athletes like Pelé who are willing to come back to the inner city and work with the kids, to help them survive.

Sometimes the exact words that a person said are separated by other words in the sentence. The other words are usually words like these:

> he said
> she cried angrily
> they shouted

Look at these sentences:

1. "I hope," she said, "you'll do as I say."
2. "Look out!" he shouted. "That car almost hit you."
3. "How can I give you a match," he asked, "when I have my hands full?"

Notice that all the exact words that a person said have quotation marks around them. The words she said, he shouted, and he asked do not. The punctuation mark that fits the tone of the words that are spoken is inside the quotation marks. A comma separates the words that tell you who is speaking.

Try It

Put quotation marks in the following sentences.

1. Oh, she said, do you eat flowers, too?
2. No! he shouted, banging his fist on the table. I won't let you do it.
3. A hen lays eggs, he said in a serious voice, because they would break if she dropped them.
4. Well, he said, that's that.
5. Eugene, she begged, stop crying.

Try It in a Paragraph

Read the story below. Decide whether or not each underlined part of the sentence is correct. If it is not, choose the correct answer from the choices at the right. Choice (a) is always the same as the underlined part in the story.

A man sat down at a snack bar and looked at the menu.

"What will you have"? asked the waiter.

"Let's see" said the man. I think I'll have the onion soup."

1. (a) | have"? asked
   (b) | have," asked
   (c) | have", asked
   (d) | have?" asked

2. (a) | see" said
   (b) | see said
   (c) | see," said
   (d) | see, said

3. (a) | man. I
   (b) | man." I
   (c) | man. "I
   (d) | man." "I

The waiter brought the soup, and the man picked up his spoon. Then he gasped. "Waiter!" he <u>shouted</u>.
⁴
"<u>There's</u> a fly in my soup!"

"Never mind, <u>sir." said</u> the waiter. "He'll only drink a
⁵
little bit."

4. (a)| | shouted. "There's

   (b)| | shouted, there's

   (c)| | shouted, There's

   (d)| | shouted." There's

5. (a)| | sir." said

   (b)| | sir" said

   (c)| | sir," said

   (d)| | sir." Said

23. CAPITAL LETTERS

LEARNING GOALS:

• To use a capital letter to begin the name of a particular person or place

• To use a capital letter to begin the name of a day of the week or holiday

• To use capitals for the first letter of important words in titles

Capital letters are used in written English to mark the beginnings of sentences, of names of people and places, of days of the week, and of many other words.

The name of a particular person begins with a capital letter: .

Henry Jones	O. J. Simpson
Superman	Billie Jean King
Bob, Ted, and José	Rosie

The name of a particular business firm or organization begins with a capital letter. The ABBREVIATIONS of these names—that is, their short forms—also begin with capitals:

the Federal Bureau of Investigation (FBI)
the Office of Economic Opportunity (OEO)
the National Association for the Advancement of
    Colored People (NAACP)
Standard Oil Company

Words like company, bureau, and university do not begin with a capital letter unless they are part of a name:

I went to work for the Brown Company.
I went to work for a large company.

I live near Ohio University.
I live near a university.

The name of a place, such as a particular city, lake, street, state, or county begins with a capital letter:

Newark	Texas
Atlantic Ocean	Harlem
Rocky Mountains	Great Lakes
Fifth Avenue	Chicago
Puerto Rico	Italy
Greece	Africa

The name of the people from a certain country or group begins with a capital letter:

French-Canadian Russian
American Indian
Sioux Chinese

The name of a region of the country begins with a capital, but words that show a direction do not:

Texas is in the Southwest.
Go west, young man.
The East is covered with smog.
He was told to walk two blocks west.

Names of the days of the week, holidays, and special events begin with capitals:

Monday Friday
Tuesday Christmas
Wednesday Thanksgiving
Thursday the Fourth of July

(Notice that the little words the and of do not begin with capital letters.)

Although holidays begin with capitals, the seasons of the year do not:

I dieted all winter and spring so I could wear
a bikini in the summer.

A person's title begins with a capital when it comes before his name, but in other cases it does not:

the Reverend Martin Luther King, Jr.
Mayor John Smith
Dr. Michael Rodriguez
Sergeant Thomas Jones
Chief White Feather
Robert Carson, the doctor
the next mayor

The first letter of important words in titles or names of books, articles, magazines, and newspapers is capitalized:

"The Women's Liberation Movement Is Growing"
(an article)

The Autobiography of Malcolm X (a book)
McCall's (a magazine)
the *New York Times* (a newspaper)

Try It in a Paragraph

Read the story below. Put capital letters wherever they are needed.

the swinging rock five had just finished playing a song to celebrate new year's day. the music was loud, but not too "together." however, the people of andersonville, california, cheered and applauded.

the weather was hot in southern california. after bowing for the applause, the players sank wearily into their seats. the guitar player wiped his forehead and asked, "what's the next number?"

"washington's march," answered the leader, bill jackson.

"good lord," said the guitar player, "i just got through playing that!"

CHECKUP TEST 4

Periods, Question Marks, and Exclamation Points

LEARNING
GOALS:

• To review
Chapters
18-23

1. Put the correct punctuation mark in each blank below.
   a. What is a draftsman____
   b. A draftsman is a person who makes drawings for engineers, architects, and designers____
   c. Great____ Do the drawings have to be exact____
   d. Yes____ They are done with compasses, slide rules, and other instruments____
   e. They must show the exact size and dimensions of the object____
   f. Wow____ What are the drawings of____
   g. Anything from toasters to space capsules, from typewriters to bridges____
   h. Heavy____
   i. It's not "heavy" if you have the proper qualifications____
   j. What are they____
   k. Draftsmen need drawing ability____
   l. They also need some training in mechanical drawing and drafting____
   m. Where is this training given____
   n. Some high schools give such training____
   o. For higher level jobs, it is usually better to take some post-high school training____
   p. Many technical schools offer such courses____
   q. Write to the American Institute for Design and Drafting, Post Office Box 2955, Tulsa, Oklahoma 74101____

Commas

2. Put commas where needed in these lists of ingredients for desserts.

   a. *Honeydew ice:* 1 cup sugar 1½ teaspoons unflavored gelatin 1½ cups water 1 very ripe honeydew melon 4 to 5 tablespoons lemon juice and food coloring.
   b. *Raspberry ice cream cake:* 1 cup cottage cheese ½ cup sugar 1 egg 1 teaspoon vanilla 2 packages frozen raspberries 1 pint vanilla ice cream 1 frozen pound cake and 1 cup heavy cream.

3. Put commas where needed in the serving suggestions for the desserts.

   Honeydew ice
   a. Form the dessert into balls.
   b. The dessert should be frozen and you should serve it as soon as you take it out of the freezer.
   c. You may serve it with slices of lemon or you may use mint sprigs.

Raspberry ice cream cake
d. Freeze until firm.
e. Lift the cake out of the pan but be sure to remove the foil.
f. Frost the top and sides.

Commas for Interrupters

4. Below is a list of words and groups of words that may be used as interrupters. From this list, choose a suitable interrupter for each sentence below, and write it in the blank in the sentence.

Albert's brother, no, yes,
a collie, please

a. _____ , I won't go.
b. Pass the butter, _____ .
c. This is Mortie, _____ .
d. _____ , Mortie is the man I told you about.
e. He owns a dog, _____ .

5. Put commas wherever they are needed in the sentences below.

a. Last night it was my turn to make dinner as usual.
b. We had cake for dessert the chocolate kind.
c. Sarah of course wanted a second helping.
d. However I didn't want her to have it.
e. As you know she is getting much too fat.
f. Freda her sister agreed with me.
g. The others who were all more tactful did not.
h. They said however that it was her own business.
i. I said, "All right go ahead."
j. "Don't blame me though when you get sick."

Commas in Dates and Places

6. Place commas where needed in the letter headings below.

a. 1400 MacDonald Avenue
   Stanford California 94307
   January 16 1978

b. 27 Elm Ridge Drive
   Salt Lake City Utah 84103
   September 20 1977

c. 61-A First Avenue
   Louisville Kentucky 40206
   March 31 1979

d. 1836 Birch Street
   New Haven Connecticut 06521
   February 14 1968

e. 205 Flower Road
   Evanston Illinois 60201
   June 11 1980

7. Place commas where needed in the sentences below.

   a. America's independence is dated from July 4 1776.
   b. In Richmond Virginia live some friends of mine.
   c. Marco is planning to move to Columbus Ohio next fall.
   d. On November 30 1978 he celebrated his twenty-fifth birth-
      day.
   e. His wife's birthday is December 2.

Quotation Marks

8. Put quotation marks, commas, periods, and question marks where needed in the sentences below.

   a. Phyllis said This is my cat
   b. His name she added is Fufu
   c. She turned to Fufu
   d. Say hello Fufu she said
   e. Meow said Fufu
   f. Then Fufu got up and walked away
   g. Phyllis asked Doesn't Fufu speak well
   h. Syd smiled
   i. He just says Meow
   j. He says it with such expression, though said Phyllis

Capital Letters

9. Tell why the words below begin with capital letters.

   a. _____ Elvis Presley
   b. _____ Boy Scouts of America
   c. _____ Oxford University
   d. _____ Wednesday
   e. _____ Texas

10. Put capital letters where needed in the sentences below.

    a. Lenny and kenny are friends.
    b. John black lives in michigan, and his aunt lives in ohio.
    c. He works for smith and company in detroit.
    d. What kind of doctor is dr. jones?
    e. In november we celebrate thanksgiving.

24. WHAT IS A SENTENCE?

Are these signs complete sentences?

Is this a sentence?

> ?putting me on you are

No, you can tell that it is not. You can read the words, but they don't make any sense. Besides, the question mark is in the wrong place, and there is no capital letter beginning the first word.

Now look at the same sentence with the words in a different order.

> Are you putting me on?

Now the same words make a sentence. Word order is one of the most important things about a sentence. Much of the meaning in a sentence depends on word order. Sentences that tell something have a different word order from sentences that ask questions.

> You are putting me on.
> Are you putting me on?

148

You know that capital letters and punctuation marks are the signs of the beginning and the end of a sentence. Even without the period and question mark in the sentences above, you would still be able to understand their meaning. The order of the words would tell you.

Try It

Put the words below in order so that each group becomes a sentence. Use the punctuation mark as a guide. Write your sentence on the blank space next to each group of words.

1. me loves He _____.
2. coffee want Do you some _____?
3. car that Watch out for _____!
4. money lost I my _____.

THE VERB

The verb is the most important part of a sentence. Verbs answer the questions:

1. What's happening?
2. When does it happen?

Without verbs, the things talked about in sentences wouldn't move, laugh, cry, talk, or even exist. The sentence would be like a movie with the action stopped.

The answer to the question "What's happening?" could be verbs like run, dance, sleep, drink, think, hope, or giggle. Or the answer could be part of the verb be. Look at the sentences below. The verbs are underlined.

> She ran to the corner.
> No, I was in the shower.
> I have worked in this factory for twenty-five
> years.
> The dog will bite the man.

As you know, some verbs have two words in them, such as have worked and will bite. The first word helps the second word tell when an action happens. But both words still just make one verb.

THE SUBJECT

Once you can answer the question "What's happening?" it's important to know who or what is doing the acting. This is the second important part of a sentence. The answer to the question "Who is doing it?" or "What is doing it?" is called the SUBJECT of the sentence.

Look at the sentences below. The subject in each sentence is underlined.

> <u>She</u> undid the chain.
> <u>Slate</u> blew his nose.
> <u>I</u> dropped my cup.
> <u>The chair</u> is standing in the corner.

You could not simply say that the noun or the pronoun in the sentence is the subject. As you can see, each sentence above has both a noun and a pronoun or two nouns. For example, the first sentence has the pronoun <u>she</u> and the noun <u>the chain</u>.

Remember, the subject tells you who is doing or who did the action. <u>The chain</u> did not do anything. <u>She</u> undid the chain. An easy way to find the verb is to ask, "What's happening?" Find the word or words that tell you. Then ask yourself, "Who or what did it?" The answer is the subject.

Try It

Underline the subject in each sentence below.

1. The fire started in the cellar.

2. Jesse threw that fast ball.

3. She is my mother-in-law.

4. The waitresses have worked in the restaurant for over three years.

5. I could only stand there and shiver.

SUBJECTS AND VERBS

You now know these two things about sentences:

1. Much of the meaning in a sentence depends on word order.
2. A sentence has two main parts: a subject and a verb.

Subjects and verbs can be put together in sentences in many different ways. Here are some of those ways:

1. A sentence may have one noun or pronoun in the subject and one verb. In the example below, one line is under the subject and two lines are under the verb.

The <u>cup</u> <u>fell</u> out of my hand.

2. A sentence may have two nouns or pronouns that make up one subject. The subject is underlined in the following example.

The <u>cup and saucer</u> fell out of my hand.

3. A sentence may have only one noun in a subject, but more than one verb. The verbs are underlined in the following example.

The cup <u>fell</u> out of my hand and <u>broke</u>.

4. A sentence may have two nouns in the subject and more than one verb.

The <u>cup and saucer</u> <u>fell</u> out of my hand and <u>broke</u>.

5. A sentence can have a subject that is not written. The subject is understood to be the pronoun <u>you</u>.

(You) Don't drop that cup!
(You) Stop it!
(You) Answer the door.

Sentences like these last three usually tell someone to do something.

Try It

In each of the sentences below, put one line under the subject and two lines under the verb.

1. The man grinned.
2. Jesse and Slate like folk rock music.
3. She undid the chain and opened the door.
4. She winked.
5. He found his hat, opened the door, and left.
6. Cola and root beer cost and taste the same at McGary's.
7. Please go to the store.
8. They left.

9. Tea and coffee taste great with cinnamon.
10. The plumber and his girlfriend drink black coffee and eat sandwiches.

WORD GROUPS THAT LOOK LIKE SENTENCES BUT AREN'T

Some groups of words look like sentences but are really only parts of sentences.

This is a sentence:

> The man who tore up parking tickets was caught.

This is not a sentence:

> The man who tore up parking tickets

The group of words, who tore up parking tickets, identifies the man. It answers the question "Which man?" The word tore is a verb, but it is used here only to help describe the man. It doesn't tell what happened to the man. The words was caught tell what happened to the man.

> The man who tore up parking tickets was caught.

In that sentence, you know which man and what happened to him. Here is another example.

This is a sentence:

> The famous man who wrote a book about marriage got divorced.

But this is not a sentence. The words below don't have a verb that tells what happened to the man.

> The famous man who wrote a book about marriage

Try It

Put a period after those groups of words that are sentences.

1. The horse that won the race is called "Lucked Out"
2. The dog, which was tied to a parking meter
3. The landlady, who hated dogs
4. The women, who were brave, whistled back at the construction workers

5. A parrot, which was always swearing
6. The store owner, who had been warned by the Health Department, made a sign that said "No Animals Allowed"
7. The cat that caught the rat
8. Citizens who read newspapers know what's happening
9. People who are grouchy
10. Who were fun

Watch out for groups of words that begin with <u>when</u>, <u>although</u>, and <u>if</u>, and are followed by a comma. When these groups of words stand alone, they are not sentences.

Here are some examples. The underlined words are part of the sentence. When they stand alone, they are not sentences.

<u>When I woke up the next morning</u>, I had a
   terrible headache.

<u>Although he found it</u>, he was still unhappy.

<u>If he hadn't lost it</u>, he would never have got-
   ten into trouble.

In each of these sentences, however, the part that comes *after* the comma *is* a sentence when it stands alone. Notice that the first letter is capitalized when the words are standing alone as a sentence:

I had a terrible headache.
He was still unhappy.
He would never have gotten into trouble.

Try It

Put a period after those groups of words that are sentences.

1. When he turned the corner, he saw her walking toward him
2. If I had you
3. Although I tried very hard
4. When the crash was heard
5. If you want to go, I'll go with you
6. When the woman went to jail
7. If they went on strike
8. When the long strike was over, they went down to McGary's and celebrated

9. Although the taxi drivers were offered a pay increase, they weren't satisfied

10. If you say yes, I'll be happy

25. VOCABULARY AND DICTIONARY SKILLS

In this chapter you will learn some ways to increase your vocabulary. You will also learn how to look words up in the dictionary.

You think and speak in words. The more words you know how to use, the more accurately you will be able to explain your ideas and feelings. Most people see, hear, and use only about 6,000 words in their lifetime. That seems like a large number, but the latest dictionary contains 600,000 words! If you are alert, your vocabulary will almost surely become larger. Each new television program, each new advertisement, each newspaper article, each new person you talk to will add new words to your personal vocabulary.

There are, of course, ways in which you may work to make your vocabulary larger on purpose. Three of these are:

1. Guessing the meaning of words as they are used in sentences.
2. Taking a word apart.
3. Using the dictionary.

WORDS IN SENTENCES

The best way to make your vocabulary larger is by looking at the way words are used in sentences. You often meet new and strange words in your reading. Don't skip over them as you would a blank space on a line. If you do, the space will always remain blank. Instead, try to figure out the meaning of the word from the words that come before and after it in the sentence.

A writer often gives you clues that help you guess the meaning of new words. The writer may define the word in the same sentence or in another sentence close by. Look at the way telecast is defined below:

> The program will be telecast throughout the country. Television viewers will see a man walk on the moon for the first time.

From the other words in the two sentences, you can guess that telecast means to send pictures and sounds by television.

Sometimes the writer may use another word in the sentence that means almost the same thing as the word you don't know. Although few pairs of words have exactly the same meaning, many words mean nearly the same thing. These words are called SYNONYMS. The word big, for example, means nearly the same thing as the words huge, gigantic, enormous, and large. Look at the way a synonym is used to define obese in the sentence below:

The fat man had a wife who was just as obese as he.

You can guess that obese means fat. If the wife was just the same as her husband, and her husband was fat, then fat and obese probably mean the same thing.

A writer will sometimes use words that have the opposite meaning to the word you don't know. Look at the way words that mean opposite things help you guess the meaning of appreciate in the sentence below:

He appreciates kindness, but he looks down on charity.

The word but is a clue that the words following it will be somewhat opposite in meaning to those in the first part of the sentence. You can guess that appreciate is the opposite of looks down on. Appreciate, then, means "think well of" or "be grateful for."

TAKING A WORD APART

Words can be taken apart to help you better understand their meanings. The body or stem of a word is called the ROOT. The root carries the basic meaning of a word. For example, the word scope is a root word. It means "to view." Some words have a part added before them called a PREFIX. Tele- is a prefix. It means "over a distance." You can add tele- to many different words:

> television—to send "vision" or pictures over a distance
> telephone—to send "sounds" over a distance
> telegraph—to send "writing" over a distance

From this, you can guess that a telescope is something that lets you "view" over a distance.

Words often have endings added to them. An ending on a word is called a SUFFIX. The ending -er means "one who does." Some words that end with -er are teacher, worker, learner, and driver.

Prefixes, which are added to the beginnings of words, and suffixes, which are added to the ends of words, can be added to many different roots. Below, you will find some words that have very common prefixes and suffixes. How many other root words can you name that use them?

Example	Root	Prefix	Meaning of Prefix
antifreeze	freeze	anti	against
depart	part	de	from
dishonest	honest	dis	not
inactive	active	in	not
preview	view	pre	before
retell	tell	re	again
submarine	marine	sub	under
supermarket	market	super	greater
unclean	clean	un	not

Example	Root	Suffix	Meaning of Suffix
terrible	terror	able, ible	capable of
formal	form	al	being like
insurance	insure	ance, ence	the act of doing something
fearful	fear	ful	full of
troublesome	trouble	some	full of, like
unity	unit (one thing)	ity, ty, y	the way something is
careless	care	less	without or lacking
movement	move	ment	the way something is
visitor	visit	or	one who does
teacher	teach	er	one who does
courageous	courage	ous	full of, or having

USING THE DICTIONARY

If you had lived two hundred years ago, you might have found this definition of cow in your dictionary:

cow: a beast well-known

The writer of the dictionary probably thought it silly to define a cow. Surely everyone knew what one was!

Today, dictionaries not only tell you what a cow is, they also tell you where the word cow comes from, how to spell cow, how to pronounce it, and how to use it in a sentence. And if you don't want to call a cow "a cow," you can usually find other names (synonyms) for it in the dictionary.

Words are placed according to the alphabet in the dictionary. This way of arranging things is called ALPHABETICAL ORDER. This means that the dictionary starts with words beginning with the letter a and ends with words beginning with the letter z. All the words beginning with the same letter are put together. The words are then placed in order by the second letter of each word. If the second letter is also the same, they are placed in order according to the third letter, and so on. Here is an example:

> am
> are
> argue
> bug
> come

Try It

Put the words below in alphabetical order.

giraffe	mustache	_____	_____
give	whiskers	_____	_____
porcupine	black	_____	_____
peekaboo	an	_____	_____
which	blanket	_____	_____

Here is a fast way to find the word you want in the dictionary. Look at the two words printed in dark letters at the top of each page. The word on the left is the first word on the page. The word on the right is the last word on the page. Because the words are in alphabetical order, you can tell whether the word you're looking for comes on that page. If it comes between the two words at the top of the page, you run your finger down that page in search of your word.

Try It

The words in List A are the words you're looking for. The words in List B are the ones in dark letters at the top of a page in the dictionary. Match the word in List A with a pair from List B to show on what page you would find each word.

List A	List B
kelp	**kvass-labellum**
open	**kick-Killiecrankie**
kiss	**kinkajou-kite**
Korea	**kook-krona**
kill	**ontogeny-open**
label	**keepsake-keratogenous**

Spelling

Of course, when you find the word you want in the dictionary, you will also see how it is spelled. If a word can be spelled two ways, the second way is given, too. If a verb changes its spelling to show past time, as swim, swam, swum, these spelling changes will also be in the dictionary. And if a noun changes its spelling when it shows more than one, as man, men, you will see the plural spelling next to the singular one. Sometimes it is in brackets [ ]. For example:

man [pl. men]

The letters "pl." mean plural, or more than one.

Some words in the dictionary are divided with a dot, as ex·hale, Her·cu·les, hand·cuff. The parts of the word separated by dots are called SYLLABLES. The dot also means that the word can be divided there with a hyphen (-) if the whole word can't fit on the end of a line.

He took a deep breath and ex-
haled slowly.

Pronunciation

Here is an example of how one dictionary shows you how to say or pronounce a word:

es·cape (ĕs·kāp′; ĭs·kāp′)

It uses special marks and letters that are always in parentheses ( ) following the word. These marks and letters come from a special alphabet called a PHONETIC ALPHABET. There is an explanation of this phonetic alphabet at the beginning of each dictionary. It tells you what sound goes with each special letter. For example, the sound ā is said like a in ape. You can also find this list of sounds on the bottom of every other page in some dictionaries. If a word can be said two ways, both pronunciations are given. Usually the first one is used more often.

Parts of Speech

The dictionary tells you what part of speech each word is. It calls words "noun," "verb," "adjective," or "adverb." You did not use all these names of words in this book, even though you saw some of them in certain sections. Here is a list of the abbreviations, or short ways to say the names, that are used in the dictionary. The abbreviation is underlined.

child, n. (noun)
he, pro. (pronoun)
laugh, v. (verb)
homely, adj. (adjective)
at, prep. (preposition)
quietly, adv. (adverb)
and, conj. (conjunction)
oh! interj. (interjection)

Usage Labels

Some words are used in special ways. The dictionary tells you how words are used by labeling them "slang," "obsolete," "colloquial," or "archaic." The label is shortened and put in brackets next to the word.

[slang] Slang means a word that is used by a group of people in the same work or way of life. It is not generally used by everyone. Some slang words are turned on, cool, pot. In time, a few slang words do become generally used. Others are forgotten.

[obs] Obsolete means a word is no longer in use, but you might see it in something written many years ago.

[archaic] Archaic means a word is rarely used. It might be found in church writings.

[colloq] Colloquial means a word is generally used in conversation or in newspapers and magazines.

If a word is not labeled slang, obsolete, archaic, or colloquial, it is considered to be generally used by everyone.

Definitions

Some words have many different meanings. Look at how the word rock is used in each of the following sentences.

Don't <u>rock</u> the boat.
Who threw that <u>rock</u>?
Put on a <u>rock</u> record.

When you look up a word in the dictionary, be sure you choose the definition that fits your sentence. There are several ways in which the dictionary helps you make the right choice.

1. As you just learned, the dictionary puts "parts of speech" labels on words. It tells whether a word is a noun, pronoun, verb, adjective, or adverb. Decide how your word is used in the sentence. Is it a noun, a verb, or a pronoun? Find the label that describes your word. Test the definition by using it in the sentence in place of the word you looked up.

2. The dictionary puts the different meanings of words in some kind of order. It may put the oldest meaning first, or it may put the most common meaning first. Be sure you read all the definitions before you choose one. You can tell how the definitions have been arranged in your dictionary by looking at the guide to the dictionary in front of the book.

Word Origins

The dictionary is also a history book. It tells you where words came from and how they were used a long time ago. The origin of a word is usually put in brackets [ ] after the pronunciation guide words.

Synonyms

Words that mean the same or nearly the same thing are called SYNONYMS. A dictionary lists the synonyms for a word near the end of the definition. Synonyms can help you talk and write more interestingly. They help you say things in different ways.

List the synonyms your dictionary gives for the following words:

cry   chew
look   pretty

26. SOME REVIEW PARAGRAPHS

LEARNING
GOALS:

• To review
all the
English skills
you have
learned
so far

On the next few pages are paragraphs and stories which review all the English skills you have learned so far. These paragraphs cover all the sections of this book. Working through the paragraphs will help you review what you have learned. If you miss an answer, go back and read that part of the book again.

Try It

Read the story below. Decide whether or not each of the underlined words is used correctly. If one is not correct, choose the correct word or words from the choices lettered (a) to (d) on the right-hand side of the page. Blacken the space next to your choice. Choice (a) is always the same as the underlined word or words in the story.

STORY 1:

This story takes place in the present.

```
        1       2      3
There are a man which worked in a factory.
```

1. (a)| | are

   (b)| | were

   (c)| | is

   (d)| | am

2. (a)| | which

   (b)| ! who

   (c)| | whose

   (d)| | when he

3. (a)| | worked

   (b)| | was working

   (c)| | had worked

   (d)| | works

One evening the guard <u>were</u> surprised to see <u>he</u>
⁴   ⁵
coming out the main gate with a wheelbarrow full of
sawdust.

4. (a)| | were

(b)| | is

(c)| | was

(d)| | are

5. (a)| | he

(b)| | her

(c)| | them

(d)| | him

The guard <u>is asking</u> him what he <u>have</u>, and the man
⁶   ⁷
says he <u>is carrying</u> a load of sawdust.
⁸

6. (a)| | is asking

(b)| | ask

(c)| | asks

(d)| | will ask

7. (a)| | have,

(b)| | has,

(c)| | had,

(d)| | got,

8. (a)| | is carrying

(b)| | carried

(c)| | was carried

(d)| | carry

<u>Him and his wife</u> are going to see if they can burn it
⁹
in the fireplace.

9. (a)| | Him and his wife

(b)| | It and his wife

(c)| | Him and her

(d)| | He and his wife

10
"Did you get permission," asks the guard.

11
Yes says the man.

12   13
"Very well," says the guard, and the man slow pushes

the wheelbarrow out the gate.

14
Not long afterward, the guard sees the man coming
15
out with another wheelbarrow who is filled with saw-

dust.

10. (a)| | permission," asks

(b)| | permission", asks

(c)| | permission?" asks

(d)| | permission"? asks

11. (a)| | Yes says the man.

(b)| | "Yes, says the
man."

(c)| | "Yes" says the
man.

(d)| | "Yes," says the
man.

12. (a)| | guard, and the man

(b)| | guard and the man

(c)| | guard, "and the
man

(d)| | guard." And the
man

13. (a)| | slow

(b)| | slowly

(c)| | slower

(d)| | slowest

14. (a)| | sees

(b)| | see

(c)| | is seeing

(d)| | saw

15. (a)| | who is

(b)| | who was

(c)| | that is

(d)| | that were

The guard asks him the same questions, and he gets
the same answers. <u>Finally</u> the guard lets the man go
                    16
on his way.

16. (a)| | Finally

    (b)| | Finally,

    (c)| | Finally.

    (d)| | "Finally,"

The man comes out with a load of sawdust for the
third time. This is <u>the most biggest</u> load he has ever
                            17
<u>took</u> out.
 18

17. (a)| | the most biggest

    (b)| | the bigger

    (c)| | the biggest

    (d)| | the more bigger

18. (a)| | took

    (b)| | take

    (c)| | takes

    (d)| | taken

The guard begins to get suspicious. He searches
through the sawdust to see whether <u>there are</u> any-
                                        19
thing valuable in it.

19. (a)| | there are

    (b)| | there is

    (c)| | there were

    (d)| | they're

<u>There isn't none</u>, and the man again is allowed to leave
      20
the gate.

20. (a)| | There isn't none,

    (b)| | There weren't
           nothing,

    (c)| | There isn't nothing,

    (d)| | There isn't
           anything,

One of the man's friends <u>say</u>, "What is this racket of
                              21
<u>your</u>?
 22

21. (a)| | say,

    (b)| | says,

    (c)| | said,

    (d)| | has said,

What are you doing with this sawdust?" The man <u>don't</u> [23]
answer.

[24]
"<u>Is</u> you stealing sawdust?" asks the friend.

[25]
"No, I <u>is</u> not stealing sawdust," says the man. "I'm
stealing wheelbarrows."

STORY 2:

This story takes place in the present.

[1]   [2]
"Harry," <u>whisper</u> the wife, poking <u>hers</u> sleeping husband.

22. (a)| | your?

   (b)| | your.

   (c)| | yours?

   (d)| | you'res?

23. (a)| | don't

   (b)| | didn't

   (c)| | do not

   (d)| | doesn't

24. (a)| | "Is

   (b)| | "Am

   (c)| | "Are

   (d)| | "Will

25. (a)| | is

   (b)| | am

   (c)| | are

   (d)| | were

1. (a)| | whisper

   (b)| | is whispering

   (c)| | whispers

   (d)| | will whisper

2. (a)| | hers

   (b)| | her

   (c)| | its

   (d)| | his

3
"Wakes up.

4   5   6
There is burglars in the kitchen and their eating mine

apple pies."

7   8
Well what do we care," says Harry, "so long like they
9
doesn't get sick in the house."

3. (a) | | "Wakes up.

   (b) | | "Woked up.

   (c) | | "Woke up.

   (d) | | "Wake up.

4. (a) | | is

   (b) | | are

   (c) | | were

   (d) | | was

5. (a) | | their

   (b) | | there

   (c) | | they're

   (d) | | theirs

6. (a) | | mine

   (b) | | his

   (c) | | their

   (d) | | my

7. (a) | | Well what

   (b) | | "Well, what

   (c) | | "Well what

   (d) | | "Well what,

8. (a) | | like

   (b) | | like that

   (c) | | as

   (d) | | as if

9. (a)|| doesn't

(b)|| isn't

(c)|| weren't

(d)|| don't

STORY 3:

This story takes place in the past.

During spring training, the baseball <u>teams</u> batting had
²
<u>be</u> very bad.

1. (a)|| teams

(b)|| team

(c)|| team's

(d)|| teams'es

2. (a)|| be

(b)|| been

(c)|| being

(d)|| beened

³
Day after day, the <u>players</u> hit poorly.

3. (a)|| players

(b)|| player's

(c)|| players'

(d)|| player

⁴   ⁵
<u>They're</u> manager <u>sits</u> on the bench and growled at
⁶
<u>they</u>.

4. (a)|| They're

(b)|| There

(c)|| Theirs

(d)|| Their

5. (a)|| sits

(b)|| sat

(c)|| is sitting

(d)|| has sat

6. (a)| | they.

(b)| | it.

(c)| | them.

(d)| | they're.

7   8
Each one tried <u>their</u> best, but <u>hardly nothing</u> worked.

7. (a)| | their

(b)| | his

(c)| | her

(d)| | its

8. (a)| | hardly nothing

(b)| | hardly anything

(c)| | hardly none

(d)| | hardly not a thing

9
Finally, unable to stand it any <u>longest</u>, the manager
10   11
rose from the dugout. He <u>grabs</u> the nearest <u>players'</u>
12   13
bat and <u>says</u>, "Look here, you guys, <u>I be showing</u> you."

9. (a)| | longest,

(b)| | long,

(c)| | longer,

(d)| | more longer,

10. (a)| | grabs

(b)| | grab

(c)| | had grabbed

(d)| | grabbed

11. (a)| | players'

(b)| | player's

(c)| | players

(d)| | player

12. (a)| | says,

   (b)| | said,

   (c)| | was saying,

   (d)| | is saying,

13. (a)| | I be showing

   (b)| | I'm showing

   (c)| | I shows

   (d)| | I'll show

14
He <u>had told</u> the pitcher to put everything he had on the ball.

14. (a)| | had told

   (b)| | tells

   (c)| | tell

   (d)| | told

15
The manager swung at the ball a number of <u>times</u> and fanned the breeze each time.

15. (a)| | times

   (b)| | time's

   (c)| | times'

   (d)| | time

16   17
After the tenth wild <u>miss. He</u> <u>throws</u> down the bat and turned to the bench.

16. (a)| | miss. He

   (b)| | miss, he

   (c)| | miss. It

   (d)| | miss! it

17. (a)| | throws

   (b)| | throwed

   (c)| | had thrown

   (d)| | threw

18
"That'll show <u>yous</u> what you jokers are doing," he shouted. "Now get in there and hit!"

18. (a)| | yous

   (b)| | yours

   (c)| | you

   (d)| | your

27. SPELLING

Learning to spell words is really much easier than it seems. Did you know that almost all the writing that is done in English uses only a small portion of the total number of words in the language? And most of these words are simple everyday words. You can probably spell many of them already.

This section will help you learn to spell the words that give you trouble. To begin with, here are four ways to help you spell a word correctly: correctly:

1. Say the word and listen to the sounds of the letters. Many words are spelled the way they sound.
2. Write the word down and see whether it "looks right" to you. After all, spelling is used only in writing. You may have learned how to spell some words without knowing it from seeing them in your reading.
3. Remember the six rules of spelling you will learn in this chapter of the book. One of these rules might fit your word.
4. Finally, check yourself by looking up the word in a dictionary. Even if you can't spell all of the word, you can probably spell enough of it to help you find it.

As you study the spelling words in this chapter, use the first two steps. Say the word and try to "see" it in your mind. Then write it down so you can see how it looks.

The words you will learn are grouped under six spelling rules. Before each group of words, you will take a short spelling test. This test covers the words you will learn. If you can spell all the words on the test correctly, you can skip the exercises for that spelling rule. If you know the words already, there's no need to spend time studying them. Go on to the next short spelling test and see how you do with those words. Whenever you get even one word wrong, stop and work through the exercises that follow the test.

You might feel better about your spelling errors if you know that most people misspell words in the same way. You could almost say that there are rules for spelling words incorrectly! The six spelling rules that follow cover some of the most common mistakes people make in spelling.

LEARNING GOALS:

- To spell words with **ie** or **ei**
- To know when to drop the last **e**
- To know when to change **y to i**
- To know when to end a word **-cede, -sede,** or **-ceed**
- To know when to double the last consonant
- To know how to indicate more than one
- To spell words that sound alike

SPELLING RULE ONE: Words with <u>IE</u> or <u>EI</u>

Test Yourself First:

Put a check next to the word in each group that is spelled correctly.

1. reciept
   receipt
   receept

2. nieghbor
   neighbor
   naighbor

3. believe
   beleive
   beleeve

4. deceet
   deceit
   deciet

Check your answers against the answers at the end of the chapter. If you got them all correct, turn to page 174.

Exercises for Words with <u>IE</u> or <u>EI</u>

About one hundred fairly common words have <u>ie</u> or <u>ei</u> in them. Many people make errors in spelling because they do not know which to use. Memorizing this well-known jingle is probably the best way to remember when to write <u>ie</u> or <u>ei</u>.

> Write i before e
> Except after c
> Or when sounded like <u>a</u>
> As in neighbor and we<u>i</u>gh.

Here are some examples of this jingle.

> "Write i before e"
> > belief
> > believe
> > piece

> "Except after c"
> > ceiling
> > receipt
> > receive

> "Or when sounded like <u>a</u>
> As in neighbor and weigh."
> > beige
> > eight
> > vein

Of the hundred or so words that have ie or ei in them, about eighty-three words are covered by the first two lines of the jingle. Only a few everyday words fall into the third group. So if you remember the first two lines, you will have learned most of the words that cause spelling errors with these letters.

Try It

Fill in the missing letters in the words below.

1. bel __ __ ve
2. perc __ __ ve
3. dec __ __ t
4. p __ __ ce
5. ach __ __ ve

6. conc __ __ t
7. rec __ __ pt
8. y __ __ ld
9. gr __ __ f
10. dec __ __ ve

Now look at the last two lines of the jingle:

"Or when sounded like a
As in neighbor and weigh."

The sound of ei in the words neighbor and weigh is like the sound of a in the word day. If you don't know whether to use ie or ei to spell a word, remember that an a sound means that you should use ei.

Try It

Fill in the missing letters in the words below.

1. w __ __ gh
2. w __ __ ght
3. fr __ __ ght

4. v __ __ n
5. r __ __ n
6. r __ __ gn

Try It Again

Check the word that is spelled incorrectly in each group below.

1. receive
   preist
   neighbor

2. reign
   beleive
   weigh

3. peice
   brief
   ceiling

4. relief
   field
   yeild

5. wieght
   vein
   achieve

SPELLING RULE TWO: Dropping the Last E

Test Yourself First:

Put a check next to the word in each group that is spelled correctly.

1. approveal
   approval
   approvl

2. including
   includeing
   includng

3. expenseive
   expensve
   expensive

4. having
   haveing
   havng

Check your answers against the answers at the end of the chapter. If you got them all correct, turn to page 176.

Exercises for Dropping the Last E

Some words drop their last e when an ending is added to them. Here are the words in the spelling test again. Each one is made up of a basic word and an ending. This shows how the endings were added:

$$approv\!\!\!/ + al = approval$$
$$includ\!\!\!/ + ing = including$$
$$expens\!\!\!/ + ive = expensive$$
$$hav\!\!\!/ + ing = having$$

Notice that each ending begins with a VOWEL, that is, with the letter a, e, i, o, or u.

The rule to remember is to drop the last e on a word if the ending you add begins with a vowel. Here are some more examples:

$$com\!\!\!/ + ing = coming$$
$$hop\!\!\!/ + ing = hoping$$
$$lov\!\!\!/ + able = lovable$$

Try It

Put the word and the ending together and write the new word on the blank line.

1. produce + ing = _____

2. desire + able = _____

3. investigate + ion = _____

4. write + ing = _____

5. make + ing = _____

6. receive + ing = _____

7. give + ing = _____

8. lose + ing = _____

9. arrive + ed = _____

10. move + able = _____

Now look carefully at the following words. Watch what happens when an ending is added.

> move + ment = movement
> care + less = careless
> hate + ful = hateful

In each of these words, the last <u>e</u> is not dropped. This is because the ending does not start with a vowel. The endings start with letters called CONSONANTS. Consonants are all letters that are not vowels. For example, the letters <u>m</u>, <u>l</u>, and <u>f</u> are consonants.

Try It

Put the word and the ending together and write the new word on the blank line.

1. state + ment = _____

2. advertise + ment = _____

3. sincere + ly = _____

4. waste + ful = _____

5. entire + ly = _____

6. safe + ly = _____

7. care + ful = _____

8. sure + ness = _____

9. refine + ment = _____

10. encourage + ment = _____

There are some words that do not follow the two rules you have just learned about dropping the last <u>e</u>. The only way to learn to spell them correctly is to memorize them.

argument	truly
judgment	wholly
acknowledgment	awful
duly	ninth
changeable	mileage

Try It

Be careful on this exercise. Remember that some words drop the last <u>e</u> when an ending is added and some words do not. Put a check next to the word in each group that is spelled correctly.

1. statment
   statement
   statemnt

2. loseing
   losng
   losing

3. arrived
   arriveed
   arrivd

4. sincerely
   sincerly
   sincerley

5. carefull
   carfl
   careful

6. movible
   moveeable
   movable

7. argument
   arguement
   argment

8. truely
   trulely
   truly

9. aweful
   awfeul
   awful

10. mileage
    milage
    milaege

SPELLING RULE THREE: Changing <u>Y</u> to <u>I</u>

Test Yourself First:

Put a check next to the word in each group that is spelled correctly.

1. accompanyed
   accompanied
   accompanned

2. easyly
   easyily
   easily

3. earliest
   earlyiest
   earlyest

4. worryed
   worried
   woried

Check your answers against the answers at the end of the chapter. If you got them all correct, turn to page 177.

Exercises for Changing <u>Y</u> to <u>I</u>

If <u>y</u> at the end of a word follows a consonant, change the <u>y</u> to <u>i</u> before adding an ending to the word. These examples show how words of this kind change when an ending is added:

$$satisfy + ed = satisfied$$
$$apply + ed = applied$$
$$enemy + es = enemies$$

Try It

1. try + ed = _____
2. pity + ful = _____
3. busy + ly = _____
4. enemy + es = _____
5. necessary + ly = _____
6. difficulty + es = _____
7. happy + est = _____
8. crazy + er = _____
9. ready + ly = _____
10. fancy + ful = _____

There is one time when you do not follow this rule. Do not change y to i if the ending that you are adding is <u>ing</u>.

cry + ing = crying
carry + ing = carrying
marry + ing = marrying

Try It

1. pity + ing = _____
2. try + ing = _____
3. study + ing = _____
4. marry + ing = _____
5. worry + ing = _____
6. reply + ing = _____

SPELLING RULE FOUR:
Is it -<u>CEDE</u>, -<u>SEDE</u>, or -<u>CEED</u>?

Test Yourself First:

Put a check next to the word in each group that is spelled correctly.

1. succeed
   succede
   sucsede

2. procede
   proceed
   prosede

3. excede
   exsede
   exceed

4. supersede
   superceed
   supercede

Check your answers against the answers at the end of the chapter. If you got them all correct, turn to page 178.

Exercises for -<u>CEDE</u>, -<u>CEED</u>, and -<u>SEDE</u>

You can easily remember which ending to write by memorizing the few words that have the endings -<u>ceed</u> and -<u>sede</u>.

Only one word ends in -sede: supersede.

Only three words end in -ceed: succeed, exceed, proceed.

All the other words end in -cede: for example, concede, precede, secede.

Try It

Fill in the missing letters.

1. suc __ __ __ __
2. pre __ __ __ __
3. pro __ __ __ __
4. super __ __ __ __
5. re __ __ __ __
6. inter __ __ __ __
7. ex __ __ __ __

SPELLING RULE FIVE: Doubling the Last Consonant

Test Yourself First:

Put a check next to the word in each group that is spelled correctly.

1. admitting
   admiting
   admiteing

2. appearing
   appearring
   appeaing

3. beginning
   begining
   begineing

4. droped
   dropeed
   dropped

Check your answers against the answers at the end of the chapter. If you got them all correct, turn to page 179.

Exercises for Doubling the Last Consonant

The next rule is somewhat difficult to remember, but it is worth spending time learning it. It covers more than three thousand words.

When you add an ending to a word, look carefully at the last two letters of the word. If the word ends in a vowel followed by a single consonant, double the consonant before you add the ending.

Here are some examples. Each word ends in a vowel followed by a single consonant (underlined).

$$\text{begin} + \text{ing} = \text{beginning}$$
$$\text{drop} + \text{ed} = \text{dropped}$$
$$\text{forget} + \text{ing} = \text{forgetting}$$

Try It

1. ship + ed = _____
2. get + ing = _____
3. swim + ing = _____
4. stop + ed = _____
5. run + ing = _____

6. plan + ed = _____
7. red + er = _____
8. occur + ed = _____
9. prefer + ed = _____
10. admit + ing = _____

Here is the second part of the rule: if the word ends in a single consonant preceded by two vowels (underlined) do not double the final consonant. Here are some examples:

$$\text{appear} + \text{ing} = \text{appearing}$$
$$\text{need} + \text{ed} = \text{needed}$$
$$\text{train} + \text{ing} = \text{training}$$

Here is the third part of the rule: If the word ends in two consonants (underlined) do not double the last consonant.

$$\text{bend} + \text{ing} = \text{bending}$$
$$\text{turn} + \text{ed} = \text{turned}$$
$$\text{insist} + \text{ed} = \text{insisted}$$

Try It Again

1. burn + ing = _____
2. refer + ed = _____
3. laugh + ing = _____
4. sing + ing = _____
5. overlap + ed = _____

6. transfer + ed = _____
7. mend + ing = _____
8. walk + ed = _____
9. beat + ing = _____
10. seem + ed = _____

SPELLING RULE SIX: Indicating More Than One

Test Yourself First:

Put a check next to the word in each group that is spelled correctly.

1. taxs
   taxes
   taxse

2. sheetses
   sheetes
   sheets

3. skies
   skyes
   skys

4. keys
   keyes
   keyies

Check your answers against the answers at the end of the chapter. If you got them all correct, turn to page 181.

Exercises for Indicating More Than One

Many people make spelling errors when they try to spell the plural of a word. Plural means "more than one." It is easy to make errors in spelling plurals because words form their plurals in many different ways. Here are five of those ways.

1. Most words form their plurals by adding s to the end of the word.

Singular	Plural
bed	beds
hat	hats
spoon	spoons
table	tables

2. Words that end in ch, sh, x, z, or s making the s sound form their plurals by adding -es:

Singular	Plural
box	boxes
church	churches
bush	bushes
glass	glasses
buzz	buzzes

3. Words ending in y after a consonant usually change y to i and add -es:

Singular	Plural
city	cities
fly	flies
library	libraries
strawberry	strawberries

4. Words ending in y after a vowel usually add s without changing the last y:

Singular	Plural
key	keys
money	moneys
toy	toys
valley	valleys

5. Words ending in <u>o</u> after a consonant often add -<u>es</u> to form the plural:

Singular	Plural
hero	heroes
mosquito	mosquitoes
tomato	tomatoes
cargo	cargoes

Try It

Write the plurals of the following words:

1. turkey _____
2. potato _____
3. car _____
4. alley _____
5. arch _____

6. tax _____
7. forty _____
8. sky _____
9. chimney _____
10. echo _____

SPELLING WORDS THAT SOUND ALIKE

Some words in English sound alike but are spelled differently. People make errors in spelling when they write one of these words but mean the other. Here are examples of some of these words:

> one, won
> right, write
> too, to, two
> sea, see

Think carefully the next time you use a word like this in a sentence. Decide which word you really mean to use so that you can spell it correctly.

Here is a list of twenty-five common words that sound alike but are spelled differently.

1. ant, aunt	10. cent, sent, scent	19. sight, site, cite
2. bare, bear	11. dear, deer	20. sole, soul
3. beat, beet	12. fair, fare	21. steal, steel
4. be, bee	13. feat, feet	22. tail, tale
5. blew, blue	14. flour, flower	23. threw, through
6. bough, bow	15. know, no	24. wait, weight
7. board, bored	16. pail, pale	25. where, ware, wear
8. brake, break	17. pair, pear, pare	
9. buy, by	18. pore, pour	

Try It

Fill in the word that best fits in the blank space in each sentence.

1. This is a (bare, bear) _____ room.

2. He (beet, beat) _____ the rug to clean it.

3. He was (board, bored) _____ by the television program.

4. Be careful not to (break, brake) _____ the glasses.

5. He wanted to go, (to, too) _____.

6. Usually only the male (deer, dear) _____ has antlers.

7. He bought (one, won) _____ book for $2.00.

8. Please get me a (pale, pail) _____ of soap and water.

9. The minister prayed for the dying man's (soul, sole) _____.

10. (Wear, Where) _____ did you put my pen?

REVIEW

Test yourself on all six spelling rules. Check the one word in each group that is spelled incorrectly.

1. receipt
   includeing
   enemies
2. begining
   lovable
   movement
3. sureness
   supercede
   admitting
4. desirable
   happiest
   piting
5. rein
   wiegh
   approval
6. neighbor
   haveing
   dropped

7. beleive
argument
proceed
8. fancyful
shopping
piece

9. shipped
taxes
appearring
10. singing
flys
occurred

Check Your Answers

TEST YOURSELF FIRST, PAGE 172

1. receipt   2. neighbor   3. believe   4. deceit

TEST YOURSELF FIRST, PAGE 174

1. approval   2. including   3. expensive   4. having

TEST YOURSELF FIRST, PAGE 176

1. accompanied   2. easily   3. earliest   4. worried

TEST YOURSELF FIRST, PAGE 177

1. succeed   2. proceed   3. exceed   4. supersede

TEST YOURSELF FIRST, PAGE 178

1. admitting   2. appearing   3. beginning   4. dropped

TEST YOURSELF FIRST, PAGE 179

1. taxes   2. sheets   3. skies   4. keys

REVIEW

Incorrect	Correct
1. includeing	including
2. begining	beginning
3. supercede	supersede
4. piting	pitying or pitting
5. wiegh	weigh
6. haveing	having
7. beleive	believe
8. fancyful	fanciful
9. appearring	appearing
10. flys	flies

ONE HUNDRED OFTEN-MISSPELLED WORDS

The following one hundred words are often misspelled. Ask someone to test you on them. Some of them you have studied in the exercises on the preceding pages; others you may already know. Practice spelling those words you don't know.

which	can't	guess	they
their	sure	says	half
there	loose	having	break
separate	lose	just	buy
don't	Wednesday	doctor	again
meant	country	whether	very
friend	February	believe	none
business	know	knew	week
many	could	laid	often
some	seems	tear	whole
been	Tuesday	choose	won't
used	wear	tired	cough
always	answer	grammar	piece
where	two	minute	raise
women	too	any	ache
done	ready	much	read
hear	forty	beginning	said
here	hour	blue	hoarse
write	trouble	though	shoes
writing	among	coming	tonight
heard	busy	early	wrote
does	built	instead	enough
once	color	easy	truly
would	making	every	straight
since	dear	through	sugar

FINAL TEST

1. Write <u>T</u> in the blank if the statement is true, and <u>F</u> if it is false.

LEARNING GOALS:

• **To test yourself on all the English skills you have learned in this book**

    a. _____ Nouns are words that name persons, places, or things.
    b. _____ <u>Sidewalk</u> is a noun.
    c. _____ Nouns may be singular or plural.
    d. _____ He is a noun.
    e. _____ <u>Doing</u> is a noun.

2. In the blank, write the pronoun from the left-hand column that may replace the words in the right-hand column. (Some pronouns may be used twice.)

    she
    they
    it
    he

    a. _____ the people
    b. _____ the house
    c. _____ the woman
    d. _____ the man
    e. _____ old Mr. Brown

3. In each sentence, underline the word that shows action.

    a. Draftsmen draw plans.
    b. They use several kinds of instruments.
    c. Many of them went to special schools.
    d. There they learned their trade.
    e. Now they have a skill.

4. Write <u>P</u> in the blank if the verb is in the present tense.

    a. _____ will jump
    b. _____ leap
    c. _____ saw
    d. _____ do
    e. _____ went

5. From the words at the right, choose the correct form of <u>be</u> for each sentence. Blacken the space next to your choice.

    a. Michael _____ a tennis player.   a. 1. || be
                                          2. || am
                                          3. || is

    b. Two champions _____ his teachers.   b. 1. || was
                                            2. || were
                                          3. || be

    c. They _____ good teachers.   c. 1. || be

2. | | were
3. | | was

d. Michael _____ good, too.

d. 1. | | were
2. | | is
3. | | am

e. Someday he _____ a champion.

e. 1. | | will be
2. | | is
3. | | be

6. In the blank beside each sentence, write the present tense of the underlined verb.

a. _____ This was Fido, my dog.
b. _____ Fido will protect my house.
c. _____ He will bark at strangers.
d. _____ He will jump at them.
e. _____ The strangers ran away.

7. Write the past tense and the past with have/has for each verb below.

Present	Past	Past with Have/Has
a. I walk	a. I _____	a. I _____
b. I know	b. I _____	b. I _____
c. I drive	c. I _____	c. I _____
d. I wear	d. I _____	d. I _____
e. I catch	e. I _____	e. I _____

8. In each sentence below, write have or has in the blank.

a. Why _____ you gone away?
b. Bertie _____ taken my dog with him.
c. We _____ seen that movie.
d. Kate and Ann _____ brought us a present.
e. It _____ been a long time.

9. In each sentence below, if both verbs show action happening at the same time, put a check mark (✔) in the blank.

a. _____ Ron steps out of the door and opens his umbrella.
b. _____ Chris opened her mouth and sings.
c. _____ They are taking their cat and leaving their dog.
d. _____ Walter will eat pie and drinks coffee.
e. _____ He likes pie and loves coffee.

10. In the blank in each sentence, write the correct verb from the left-hand column. (Some verbs may be used twice.)

   is   a. Bill and John _____ friends.
   are   b. Money _____ useful.
   vote   c. The committee _____ for new rules.
   votes   d. Arthur and Nellie _____ in every
                   election.
                 e. Gloria, Cheryl, and Kay _____, too.

11. Underline the word in parentheses that should be used in each sentence.

   a. One of the waiters (serve, serves) the soup.
   b. Everybody (like, likes) ice cream.
   c. One of the people in the room (stand, stands) up.
   d. All my friends (has, have) cars.
   e. Neither Gladys nor Stan (is, are) here.

12. In each blank, write the correct pronoun from the column on the left.

   myself   a. We can do it _____.
   yourself   b. He wanted to go by _____.
   himself   c. I bought _____ a new coat.
   itself   d. Behave _____!
   ourselves   e. That cat washed _____.

13. In each sentence, write who, which, or that in the blank.

   a. The man _____ came to dinner stayed too long.
   b. This is the house _____ Jack built.
   c. I stained my shirt, _____ I just got back from the
      laundry.
   d. The birds _____ are singing are in the trees.
   e. This is the book _____ you wanted to read.

14. In each sentence, underline the word in parentheses that is correct.

   a. He is taller than (I, me).
   b. Marty is a better athlete than (they, them).
   c. You are sorrier for him than for (she, her).
   d. He is angrier at himself than at (they, them).
   e. She works harder than (he, him).

15. Put a check mark (✔) in the blank before the sentences that are correct.

   a. _____ This is just between you and me.
   b. _____ Come to the party with Kenneth and I.

c. _____ Don't blame it on me.

d. _____ A jar of cookies were on the shelf.

e. _____ Ben told Judy about them.

16. Put -ly on each word that tells how the action happened.

   a. The shabby old man walked slow.
   b. Sudden he saw a dollar bill in the street.
   c. He ran to it quick.
   d. Smiling joyful, he picked it up.
   e. He walked on brisk.

17. In each blank, write the correct pronoun from the left-hand column.

   her
   its
   my
   whose
   your

   a. I like to leave _____ feet bare.
   b. _____ book is this?
   c. Have you finished _____ work?
   d. The house is pretty, but _____ walls are bare.
   e. Every woman was doing _____ thing.

18. Put an apostrophe where needed in the sentences below.

   a. Why are firemens suspenders red?
   b. Alices hair is curly.
   c. Teachers aides are sometimes called paraprofessionals.
   d. The rabbits tail was white.
   e. The childrens toys were scattered around the room.

19. Write the contraction for each group of words below.

   a. _____ are not
   b. _____ does not
   c. _____ they are
   d. _____ who is
   e. _____ it is

20. Put a check mark (✔) next to the sentences below that are correct.

   a. _____ I hardly never go there.
   b. _____ Nobody hasn't any.
   c. _____ John has scarcely any money.
   d. _____ Rubin cannot do no better.
   e. _____ Anything he wants, he gets.

21. Underline the word in parentheses that should be used in each sentence.

   a. (Lie, Lay) your head on my shoulder.
   b. This is different (from, than) the other tests.

    c. I could (have, of) danced all night.
    d. Do you have anything (farther, further) to say?
    e. It sounds (like, as) a bargain.

22. Put the correct punctuation mark at the end of each sentence below.

    a. Hurry ____
    b. Watch out ____
    c. Who has the camera ____
    d. Have you seen my pictures ____
    e. Edmund took them ____

23. Put commas where they are needed in the following lists.

    a. cucumbers radishes and tomatoes
    b. apples pears peaches and apricots
    c. sugar and spice
    d. men women or children
    e. art architecture and photography

24. Mark <u>X</u> in the blank next to the sentences where commas are missing.

    a. _____ Harry and Pete are friends.
    b. _____ They go to baseball games, and they also like hockey.
    c. _____ Once they took me to a football game but I didn't like
             it.
    d. _____ The field was muddy and my team lost.
    e. _____ Next time my team will win or I won't go.

25. Underline the interrupters in the following sentences.

    a. Lisa, my cousin, didn't like dogs.
    b. However, she wanted a pet of her own.
    c. In fact, she chose a bird.
    d. The bird, a blue one, flew away.
    e. Lisa misses Pandora, her bird.

26. Put commas where needed in the dates and addresses below.

    a. January 31 1982
    b. President Carter
       1400 Pennsylvania Avenue
       Washington D.C.
    c. Craig lives at 62 Elm Lane Pittsburgh Pennsylvania.
    d. He was born in May 1958.
    e. On May 10 1959 he was one year old.

27. Put quotation marks and a comma where needed in the sentences below.

    a. Freda said Give me your hand.

b. I asked her Why?
c. I want to manicure it she answered.
d. When we came to their door, they shouted Welcome!
e. Thank you we said.

28. Put quotation marks where needed in the sentences below.

    a. As for me, Alec said, I play the drums.
    b. How interesting! Betty exclaimed. Do you play in a band?
    c. No, he answered. I play for myself.
    d. Someday she said, I would like to hear you.
    e. Fine! he said. How about now?

29. Underline the correct form of the word or words in parentheses.

    a. John works for the (Fbi, FBI).
    b. He is an (Agent, agent).
    c. He works in (Washington, D.C., Washington, D.c.).
    d. He has (Tuesdays, tuesdays) off.
    e. He gets a vacation in the (Summer, summer).

30. Put capitals where needed in the sentences below.

    a. elections were held in november.
    b. I voted for harvey brown for mayor.
    c. However, mayor thompson was reelected.
    d. I forget if he is a republican or a democrat.
    e. On election day he had a party.

31. Put a check mark (✓) in the blank next to each group of words that is a sentence.

    a. _____ Robin's new dress.
    b. _____ The dress that I saw in the window.
    c. _____ I like that dress.
    d. _____ Who are you?
    e. _____ As he walked slowly down the block.

32. Put one line under the subject and two lines under the verb in the sentences below.

    a. He fell.
    b. The boy fell on the sidewalk.
    c. He hurt his knee.
    d. Jenny and Jessie visited their neighbor.
    e. Later, they went home.

33. Match a prefix or suffix from column 1 and a root from column 2 to make the word defined in column 3. Write the word in the blank space.

Prefix or Suffix	Root	Definition	Word
sub	farm	a. not polite	a. _____
ible	polite	b. under the earth	b. _____
im	horror	c. get again	c. _____
er	terranean	d. full of horror	d. _____
re	gain	e. one who farms	e. _____

34. List the words below in alphabetical order.

blood, block, brain, blond, braid

a. _____
b. _____
c. _____
d. _____
e. _____

35. Fill in the missing letters in the words below.

a. bel __ __ ve
b. rec __ __ pt
c. w __ __ gh
d. satisf __ ed
e. enem __ __ s

36. Put a check mark (✔) in the blank next to the words that are spelled correctly.

a. _____ having
b. _____ desireable
c. _____ safly
d. _____ succeed
e. _____ beginning

Read each story below and decide if each of the underlined words or group of words is used correctly. If one is not correct, choose the correct word or words from the lettered choices on the right-hand side of the page. Blacken the space next to your choice. Choice (a) is always the same as the underlined word or words in the story.

STORY 1:

David Pearson outraced Cale Yarborough's challeng-
ing Oldsmobile to win the Firecracker 400 today by

1. (a) ‖ than
   (b) ‖ from

1
less <u>than</u> a car length.

(c) | | then

(d) | | as

2
Pearson came up behind <u>Baxter Price's</u> slower Chevrolet on the final turn, paused a few seconds, and then pulled around him on the outside.

2. (a) | | Baxter Price's

   (b) | | Baxter Prices

   (c) | | Baxter's Price

   (d) | | Baxter Prices'

3
"He [Yarborough] <u>don't</u> see him until I pulled out
4
and around <u>him</u>" said the 43-year-old five-time winner of the event.

3. (a) | | don't

   (b) | | didn't

   (c) | | doesn't

   (d) | | hasn't

4. (a) | | him"

   (b) | | him."

   (c) | | him,"

   (d) | | him.

5
Pearson, <u>who</u> won $12,625 for his drive and additional money in contingency prizes, said he had no intention of "hiding" Price's car from Yarborough's
6
view. But <u>that in fact</u> is what happened.

5. (a) | | who

   (b) | | which

   (c) | | that

   (d) | | whom

6. (a) | | that in fact

   (b) | | that in fact,

   (c) | | that, in fact

   (d) | | that, in fact,

Pearson said Yarborough's mistake $\underset{7}{\underline{is}}$ trying to pass $\underset{8}{\underline{he}}$ on the inside instead of the outside. Yarborough said after the race he was "surprised" to come upon Price's car and called Pearson's move "a good tactic."

7. (a) | | is

   (b) | | are

   (c) | | was

   (d) | | were

8. (a) | | he

   (b) | | him

   (c) | | her

   (d) | | them

STORY 2:

Grandma Prisbrey $\underset{1}{\underline{be}}$ pleased about $\underset{2}{\underline{she's}}$ recent recognition as a folk $\underset{3}{\underline{artist}}$ $\underset{4}{\underline{but}}$ $\underline{she's}$ puzzled that people $\underset{5}{\underline{has}}$ $\underline{come}$ to think of $\underset{6}{\underline{her}}$ hobby $\underset{7}{\underline{like}}$ $\underline{art}$.

1. (a) | | be

   (b) | | is

   (c) | | been

   (d) | | had been

2. (a) | | she's

   (b) | | hers

   (c) | | its

   (d) | | her

3. (a) | | artist but

   (b) | | artist but,

   (c) | | artist, but

   (d) | | artist. but

4. (a) | | she's

   (b) | | her

(c) | | shes

(d) | | hers

5. (a) | | has come

(b) | | have come

(c) | | has came

(d) | | have came

6. (a) | | her

(b) | | hers

(c) | | her's

(d) | | shes

7. (a) | | like

(b) | | as

(c) | | like as

(d) | | as if

"They call me an artist, even though I cant draw a
                                               8
car that looks like one." she says. "But you know, I
                9   10
guess there's all different kinds of art."
       11   12

8. (a) | | cant

(b) | | cann't

(c) | | can't

(d) | | cannt

9. (a) | | one."

(b) | | one,"

(c) | | one"

(d) | | one

10. (a) | | says

(b) | | say

(c) | | sayed

(d) | | will say

11. (a) | | there's

(b) | | there is

(c) | | there are

(d) | | it's

12. (a) | | kinds of

(b) | | kinds a

(c) | | kind of

(d) | | kinda

INDEX

ACKNOWLEDGMENTS

The advice and contributions of the following educators are gratefully acknowledged: Angelica W. Cass, The City College, City University of New York; Philip W. Loveall, Maine Township High School East, Park Ridge, Illinois; Joseph J. Brain, Technical Director of the English Teaching Faculty Program for the New York Junior League; Mildred Love, New York Manpower Development Training Program; George D. Crothers, The City College, City University of New York; Judith Babbitts, Educational Systems Corporation, Washington, D.C.